KU-692-862

THE COMMON MARKET

THE COMMON MARKET

J. F. DENIAU

LONDON
BARRIE AND ROCKLIFF
WITH
PALL MALL PRESS

English translation by Graham Heath
from the French edition entitled
Le Marché Commun
(Published 1959 by Presses Universitaires
de France, Paris)

by Barrie and Rockliff (Barrie Books Ltd.)
and Pall Mall Press Ltd.,
2 Clement's Inn, London WC2
Second Edition 1961
Third Edition 1962
Reprinted 1963

Printed in Great Britain by
THE STELLAR PRESS LTD
Union Street, Barnet, Herts.

Contents

Contents (continued)

THE COMMON MARKET

INTRODUCTION

From Politics to Economics

THE Common Market Treaty, which was signed at Rome on March 25th 1957 between France, Germany, Italy, the Netherlands, Belgium and Luxembourg, marks the convergence of two trends which have appeared in Europe and the world since the end of the War: the growth of political awareness and the pressure of economic necessity.

Even before the end of hostilities it had become clear to a number of thoughtful people that Europe's political compartmentalisation, far from being a sign of vitality and a guarantee of full opportunity for each country, was a source of enfeeblement and decline. Hence it was in London, before the liberation of Belgium, Holland and Luxembourg, that a psychological rapprochement was born which first manifested itself in the establishment of Benelux.

With the coming of peace it became even clearer that the world's destiny lay in the hands of two great powers, the United States and the U.S.S.R., and that in this dialogue the individual countries of Europe could only make their voices heard by allying themselves with one or other of the great powers.

Europe was trying to find itself, all the more so because Europe was no longer its former self. Geographically the eastern half had been amputated and had fallen under Soviet sway. At the same time the western half, covered with the ruins of war, found its traditional mission overseas being challenged at Bandoeng. Hungary and Suez were two unmistakable signs of this dual retreat, both material and moral.

And so a vague idea gradually gained ground that it was no longer enough to be a Frenchman, a German or an Italian; nor was the thought of being an American or a Russian any more satisfying. This quest for European unity with the far-sighted and tenacious support of the United States, which realised that the fragmentation of Europe was a dangerous source of political instability, gave rise to a vast number of ventures and organisations; ventures instigated by private individuals, trade unions, governments and parliamentarians; organisations representing every shade of political opinion, every walk of life and every religious persuasion.

These post-war manifestations of the European idea form an impressive list, even in summary form. Some were a revival of earlier efforts, like those of Count Coudenhove-Kalergi, while others were entirely new departures. There was the United Europe Movement; the French Council for United Europe; the European League for Economic Co-operation; the New International Groups (which had a Christian basis); the Socialist Movement for the United States of Europe; the European Union of Federalists; the European Commons' Council; the European Parliamentary Union; the European Movement; the Committee of Action for the United States of Europe; the Vigilance Committee for Europe; etc. Amongst the personalities directing or co-ordinating these movements there were some names which reappeared frequently regardless of their political affiliations or nationality: Guy Mollet, Bech, Adenauer, de Gasperi, Beyen, Schuman, Spaak and Jean Monnet. In addition there were a whole series of ventures among trade unionists, professional and cultural groups, which encouraged study, personal contacts and rapprochements under the name of 'Europe'.

But although there was general agreement on the word 'Europe' there were still differences and doubts as to the nature of the Europe which was to be created, its extent and its scope. There was no agreement, no common ground between the protagonists of *laissez-faire* and of planning; between those who put their faith in parliamentary action and those who preferred to appeal directly to public opinion; between those who, like the English, favoured diplomatic co-operation without any surrender of sovereignty and those others who were working towards the creation, in one form or another, of a union, a United States of Europe, or a Federation. The Council of Europe, which was set up in 1949, embraced fifteen European countries, and all shades of opinion were represented in its Consultative Assembly at Strasbourg, but it often merely served to confirm these dissensions.

After the frustration of the attempts to establish the primarily political community in 1953 some of the prime movers of the European movement deliberately turned their backs on the ideal of building a Europe of fifteen or seventeen nations; an ideal which had proved too complex and too wide to prevent the sum of the divergent national interests from triumphing every time over the sum of the positive common factors. Instead, they turned their efforts towards a more technical and more restricted field, that of six geographically adjacent continental countries which were closely linked both psychologically and economically and equally determined to seek out the most constructive solutions. This is what has sometimes been ironically referred to as 'little Europe', forgetting that it is the heart of the continent and contains two-thirds of its free population. It is certainly a limited Europe, but this circumscription gives it greater strength. As long ago as 1950 Robert Schuman had made his historic proposal for the formation among these six countries of a Coal and Steel 'Pool', which pointed the way to a new European order based particularly on a Franco-German rapprochement. The failure of the European Defence Community placed a temporary check on this development but ultimately confirmed the soundness of its economic aims, which were on less dangerous psychological ground and were undeniably useful.

At the end of hostilities the Allied Powers had laid down in the Havana Charter some principles to be applied in international economic relations. These principles were based on two lines of thought; that co-operation was essential and that the ultimate aim should be the liberation of trade.

The protectionist policies which had operated for more than half a century and had been intensified in the inter-war period, had left a threatening legacy of confusion and instability in the world's economy. Apart from a few small countries which were either highly competitive in certain industries or specialised as brokers or converters of the products of other countries, international trade had to contend with an economy which was broken up into innumerable water-tight compartments and saddled with all kinds of currency controls, tariff barriers and, in particular, quantitative restrictions on imports. The balance-of-payments problems and the needs of economic reconstruction, which are characteristic of all post-war periods, inevitably aggravated these restrictions. Again with the support of the United States, a powerful movement began to take shape for the restoration of commercial and economic relations in accordance with the theories which assert that international competition in a really big market will ensure that men and materials are put to the best use.

It was in Europe that this movement was to achieve its greatest results, for it was the protectionism and the economic and financial instability of Europe which most clearly showed the need for it. In 1948 the Benelux economic and customs union came into force between Belgium, the Netherlands and Luxembourg. But it was General Marshall's Harvard speech of June 5th 1947 which was destined to have the widest results, leading as it did to the establishment of the Organisation for European Economic Co-operation (O.E.E.C.).

Within the framework of the O.E.E.C., which embraced all the countries of Western Europe, very substantial progress had been made in the easing of currency restrictions and more generally in the solution of problems of foreign trade. But the failure in 1955 of an attempt to tackle the actual question of customs tariffs gave further evidence of the limits of traditional intergovernmental cooperation.

The effective fusion of markets through economic integration seemed a more coercive but more certain way of increasing trade and raising living standards. To it was added the idea of a pooling of resources and a co-ordination of effort. These ideas, which were difficult to put into practice on a general basis, were first tried out in separate sectors, commencing with the European Coal and Steel Community (E.C.S.C.) which brought the six countries of the Common Market together for the first time. Other projects followed.

But it soon became evident that integration by sectors could only yield limited results. Its restricted scope, unconnected with the other parts of the economic and financial system, ruled out any large-scale activities and made it impossible to achieve an overall equilibrium. To sweep away from Europe protectionism and economic nationalism, with their resulting high production costs, high costs of living and economic stagnation, a different approach was required, a wide attack in more than one dimension as it were; it must have the depth of integration and the wide scope of a freeing of trade. This approach was provided first by the Beyen Plan and then by the Spaak Report, which marked the first step towards the Common Market.

We must define this modest and almost commercial term 'Common Market' which bids fair to become a proper name.

G.A.T.T. (General Agreement on Tariffs and Trade), a specialised agency for world trade with its headquarters in Geneva, provides for two types of deliberate expansion of markets: one is the free trade area, in which each participant maintains its own tariffs against non-members, and the other is the customs union in which, in addition to removing all trade barriers between themselves, the Member States establish a common tariff against third parties. The Treaty of Rome goes further. It is a customs union in which attention has been devoted not only to the barriers between the states but also to the effective balance of strength between the participants, and to the economic, financial and social reactions which may take place within each member state. In short, however paradoxical it may seem, the attainment of a Common Market has involved a painstaking search for a solution to the problems of each nation, as well as to many problems which are not strictly concerned with trade.

The Treaty of Rome, which established the Common Market, thus marks the convergence of two movements which have appeared in Europe since the end of the War; a political movement towards international rapprochement and an economic movement towards the expansion of markets.

Other approaches to the necessary expansion of markets are doubtless possible in other circumstances. But there is no doubt that the provisions of the Treaty of Rome as a whole are not merely the fortuitous outcome of negotiations. They do not merely reflect a balance between the political views of the six countries which wished to go 'faster and farther' towards European co-operation; they also represent the triumph of a theory and a lesson drawn from experience.

PART I

From the Theory of the Large Market to the Common Market Treaty

CHAPTER ONE

The Theory of the Large Market

THE concept of a market is a relatively new one; or rather it is a concept which is now enjoying a revival after long periods of eclipse. A market is in the first instance a place of sale, and certain ancient and privileged places of sale played a dominant role in the rise of urban trade in the Middle Ages. But gradually the merchant economy, best exemplified in the great European trade fairs and the many wealthy merchant cities, ports or route centres, gave place to a producers' economy. The nineteenth century, which marked the culmination of this evolution, concentrated its attention on the problems of production and in particular on the development of the means of production. The twentieth century saw the attention of economists swing away from production proper to the marketing of goods.

It was no longer the captain of industry, the 'ironmaster' who held the stage as the prime mover of progress; it was the consumer, whose conscious or unconscious decisions determined the direction and volume of trade.

There was less emphasis on production possibilities and more on production for a given market. The end to be achieved reacted on the means to be employed: the decisive factor in drawing up plans, establishing investment programmes and organising the economy was now the existence of a certain purchasing power, directed and distributed in particular ways. The market governed individual choices and, to a large extent, the trade cycles.

But the term 'market' had been changed and considerably extended. Originally it meant the particular place – a market-place or building – in which trading was conducted on a particular day. Today the term 'market' means the number of potential purchasers for a particular product sold under particular conditions. These conditions include every possible factor: the selling price, the distribution of the purchasers, the available means of distributing the product and the obstacles of geography, psychology, finance, tariffs and administration which hinder that distribution. Thus, the bounds of time and place have been shattered and can be enormously extended; but the unity on which the market is now based is provided by the existence of purchasers who, though scattered in time and space, are all of them ready to purchase a given product at a given price. At the same time, the question of securing a certain equality of access to the consumer acquires great importance.

In the nineteenth century the liberal system of international trade had masked the importance of this factor. The theory laid particular stress on the advantages of an international division of labour as a means of promoting trade and raising the standard of living. The idea of a market in its present sense had not yet crystallised, the economic unity of the world being sufficiently guaranteed by complete freedom of trade; it was a unity, moreover, which included the free movement not only of goods but also of capital, investments and labour, and the convertibility of currencies. But the liberal mechanisms of world trade were challenged, both in fact and in theory, as the problems of the balance of payments and the economic growth of the under-developed countries assumed dominating proportions. All kinds of restrictions were placed on the various facilities which are the concomitants of free trade: the free movement of capital and labour and the free exchange of currency. And so the idea of a definite geographical area within which there was a certain unity in the conditions of trade (in the widest sense) regained all its old importance; and it was within the frontiers of the individual country that it first became effective, as commercial restrictions came to buttress the political barriers.

Attention was redirected to the limits set by economic frontiers at the very moment when a deliberately consumer-biassed economy was developing within the largest national units such as the United States. The question of the size of the market could no longer be overlooked by economic theory. Henceforth it had to be treated as one of the factors determining the structure of industry and the viability of an economy.

THE TECHNICAL ADVANTAGES OF THE LARGE MARKET

When markets are split up into units which are too small, owing to political conditions or to deliberate protectionism, the advantages which can justifiably be expected from technological progress are in practice wiped out or withheld. It is thus possible to speak of the drawbacks of a restricted market or the advantages of a large market.

The drawbacks of a restricted market are that the modern potentialities of production and distribution cannot be used to the full. On the other hand, only a larger market appears able to give full scope for research, productivity, lower production costs and increased consumption.

The technical advantages of a large market lie first and foremost in the organisation of production and in the structure of industry. A large market opens the way to mass production – the manufacture of a particular type of product at a constant flow and in very large numbers. It is thus possible to ensure that machinery and equipment are fully employed. In an economy which is split up into small units – as is the case in Europe today – machinery is in effect unemployed, sometimes for as much as eighteen hours out of twenty-four, as for instance in the textile industry. Another example is provided by the small market for agricultural products in France, which contributes to the high cost of tractors. A further benefit of mass production is that it enables manufacturers to cut down those overhead charges which do not increase in proportion to output. This is the case with trading and marketing expenses, stockholding, research and planning. The same applies to financial charges, since large firms are usually able to borrow money on more favourable terms than small ones.

The advantages which accrue to industry internally are matched by benefits arising from the degree of specialisation which only a huge market permits. Moreover, a firm which is assured of a large number of consumers can enjoy the advantages of specialisation without necessarily increasing its size. In the small Belgian market, for instance, it is uneconomic to set up a complete motor industry, whereas in a larger market it would be well worth while for Belgium to take a hand in one of the processes of the industry such as assembly. The specialisation of workers and staff, of equipment and tools, and of marketing channels, contribute both to the full employment of men and machines, just as in mass production, and to their more rational use from the point of view of efficiency and lower production costs. In particular, a large and steady market for a specialised firm is an essential prerequisite for any serious attempt at staff training and industrial or scientific research, measures which are of such great importance in modern industry; low or irregular output, on the other hand, will not meet the outlay of time and money required to introduce them and recover their cost.

THE ECONOMIC ADVANTAGES OF THE LARGE MARKET

Mass production and specialisation tend to reduce production costs substantially, but this reduction will not be reflected in lower selling prices so long as the producer is protected. It is only competition which will ensure that all the benefits accruing to the producer from the existence of a large market will be passed on to the consumer. But a market of this type does in fact increase the possibilities of competition. There is less likelihood of scarcity value, there are more opportunities for competition, it is less easy for a producer to eliminate his competitors or come to an agreement with all of them and thus secure control of the whole market. Only in a large market is it possible for big firms to develop freely under conditions of free competition. By reviving and intensifying competition a large market is therefore a factor in economic progress and the raising of living standards.

A large market, besides enabling industry to adopt the most up-to-date and economic production systems, ensures a better distribution of functions between different regions. By guaranteeing the free movement of raw materials, manpower and capital, as well as of goods, it tends to bring the distribution of economic activity into line with the requirements of productivity. The borrowing of money becomes easier. There is less fluctuation in marketing, and hence less uncertainty attaches to expansion, particularly in the case of agriculture. Industries such as atomic power and civil aviation, which it would be prohibitive, or at least very expensive, to operate in a limited market, become viable. This pooling of markets, backed by a pooling of resources, is a decisive factor in hastening economic growth.

The full employment of machines, mass production, specialisation, exploitation of the latest technical discoveries, a revival of competition – all these factors tend to reduce production costs and selling prices. In addition there is the possibility of a net reduction of one element of the price through the abolition of customs duties. The result should be an increase of purchasing power and a rise in the real standard of living. The increased number of consumers of a particular product should thus permit an increase in consumption and hence a greater increase in investment.

Economic expansion then begins to snowball. Increased consumption brings increased investment, increased investment enables prices to be lowered and wages increased, leading to an overall increase in purchasing power. In the compartmentalised economies of the post-war period systematic efforts have been made to achieve this economic expansion; it seems, however, that in a restricted market, with limited possibilities of production, there is always a danger of financial instability, and that only a substantial increase in the size of the market can hasten and stimulate expansion.

CHAPTER II

The History of Large Markets

DOES the history of large markets bear out the theoretical advantages attributed to them? Not entirely. In the first place, political considerations and objectives have always played a large part in the establishment of large markets, so that it is not easy to pick out the purely economic factors. Secondly, previous attempts to put theory into practice have given rise to undeniable difficulties which had not been allowed for in theory; in the recent past those difficulties have been sufficient to wreck even the attempt to establish a large market.

An early form of expanded market was that of an existing political framework within which trading conditions were unified. In France, as early as the seventeenth century, Colbert abolished certain internal customs barriers in order to cure local shortages. Turgot's edicts, particularly that dealing with the free movement of grain, completed Colbert's work and laid the foundation for the full economic unification of France, which went hand-in-hand with political unification. Similarly in Great Britain in the eighteenth century the trammels on internal trade were steadily removed and the work of economic unification was carried forward alongside the political unification of England, Scotland and Ireland, thanks to the stimulus given by economists like Adam Smith who regarded the process as an essential condition for an increase of wealth. In Switzerland economic unification took place naturally, if somewhat belatedly, in the second half of the nineteenth century through the abolition of cantonal tolls. Similarly in the new countries of Australia, Canada or South Africa, internal economic unification and the establishment of a customs union came about as the normal consequences of political unity and were achieved without difficulty.

But in countries where political unity was insecure or disputed, economic unification was equally insecure if not a total failure. In the Austro-Hungarian Empire, in addition to political and racial strife, there was a constant antagonism between Hungary, with its agricultural and liberal economy, and Austria, which was industrial and protectionist, with the result that a satisfactory balance was never established between their two markets. Similarly Sweden and Norway, although politically united for almost a century from 1815 to 1897, never managed to create a united market. Their political separation into two independent states automatically brought about an economic separation. It therefore seems that even within an existing political framework the home market can only be successfully unified if there is a strong common will to achieve that unification.

This question of political will crops up again in the case of an expansion of markets accompanying the establishment of a federation or confederation of states. Here it is no longer a matter of internal measures; negotiations must be undertaken with the aim of bringing the partners together politically and economically at the same time. History shows that in such cases the two processes are intimately linked and virtually interdependent. Political union by itself soon proves impracticable without a corresponding economic union; economic union is only feasible if the States – or one of them – include it in their political programme.

THE UNITED STATES OF AMERICA

The example of the United States shows how a union which was originally envisaged as being purely political soon had to be strengthened by the ties of trade. Neither the Declaration of Independence of July 4th 1776 nor the Constitution ratified by the thirteen States in 1781 contain any provisions authorising the Federal Government to regulate trade between the States. This lack of economic unity quickly gave rise to serious complications in trade and dissatisfied several of the less-favourably situated States which were suffering economically. Hence the Constitution of 1787 removed from the individual States the right to keep their own tariffs and currencies. *Article 8* lays it down that Congress alone shall have the right to regulate trade with foreign countries. *Article 9* states that no commercial or fiscal preferences shall be accorded to the ports of one State to the detriment of the ports of another. *Article 10* states that no State shall levy taxes or duties on imports or exports without the consent of Congress. The constitutions of the States which were created and brought into the Union in the nineteenth century showed the same anxiety to achieve a united and free home market under the control of federal institutions; a manifestation of this tendency which still exists today is the Inter-State Commerce Commission, set up in 1887 and directly responsible to the President and to Congress.

The United States had been quick to realise that political unity must be buttressed by a unified home market and that a unified and expanded market was essential to the development of their prosperity, yet in practice their difficulties were not all over. For a long time there was opposition between the agricultural south, wedded to free trade, and the north, with its industrial and protectionist economy, and the Civil War was to a large extent an economic conflict. It was only the advent of the most recent technical developments in the production and distribution of power supplies, particularly through petroleum, that some areas were enabled to share in the growing prosperity of the United States and a satisfactory balance was established.

THE ZOLLVEREIN

The establishment of the Zollverein (customs union) in nineteenth century Germany shows a different example of a political union linked with an economic union. The decisive factor in this case was a political will, that of Prussia. But the unified market, instead of being a consequence of a political union, was the means chosen to attain the desired political end. At the opening of the century Germany consisted of some forty tiny States separated by innumerable tariff walls of varying heights. Under these conditions the industries which had sprung up in response to Napoleon's Continental Blockade were unable to withstand the competition of England. The larger and more advanced of the German States felt the need to increase their economic strength by enlarging their home markets. The first suggestion came from Bavaria in 1819, but it was the remarkable pertinacity of Prussia over more than half a century which finally brought about the customs union. Initially the idea of a customs union between the German states had been rejected on account of the wide disparities in their levels of development and in the nature of their economies; some were agricultural, some industrial; some orientated their trade towards England, others towards Austria or Russia. The most that had been achieved was the recognition of the principle of bilateral negotiations for facilitating trade. Prussia's first step was to secure the free movement of goods within its own provinces; this was to be an example of a liberal trade policy which would infect neighbouring States with the irresistible contagion of a free and unified market. These expectations were soon fulfilled. Three local customs unions were formed in Germany, and Prussian policy then turned to the task of breaking down the local customs unions and joining them step by step to a general customs union, the Zollverein.

From 1834 to 1867 the Zollverein provided a free home market and a common tariff against other countries under the control of a customs conference in which each State had one vote and decisions had to be taken unanimously. The rule of unanimity paralysed the development of the Zollverein, however, and in 1867 a new treaty replaced it by a dual authority: a federal executive composed of governmental representatives, and a legislative body made up of representatives elected by direct universal suffrage. Finally, in 1871, these bodies were transformed into permanent organs of the German Empire.

The Zollverein experiment is interesting from a number of points of view. In the first place, it showed that a widening of the market resulted in a substantial economic expansion; many other provinces besides Prussia were able to establish or develop industries which had hitherto been moribund. Specialisation benefited the spinning industry in Saxony, the breweries of Bavaria and the manufacturing industries of Silesia. The general upturn in economic activity, under the stimulus of the expanded market, brought a striking increase in the demands for coal and for the products of the basic industries in general. Large-scale improvements of communications, roads and ports were set in hand. There was a rapid and unmistakable rise in the general standard of living. The Zollverein experiment was interesting from another point of view; being undertaken in the nineteenth century it reflected some of the economic principles of the period. Unity was equated primarily with freedom, i.e., the mere abolition of existing barriers. As the European economy was in a stage of rapid expansion, this freeing of trade could be effected without any repercussions beyond an increase in specialisation. Lastly, the history of the Zollverein shows the absolute necessity of an unswerving political will.

As long as the Zollverein was operated by a sort of permanent negotiation between sovereign states protected by the rule of unanimity, decisions on commercial and economic matters were very difficult to reach and in practice ineffective, even when the negotiations were carried on at the highest political level, and the crisis of 1867 showed the decisive role of political institutions during the period of formation of a customs union.

THE UNIFICATION OF ITALY

The undeniable success of the unification of the German market, from the economic point of view, must not blind us to the difficulties and risks inherent in such a process even when it follows in the wake of a powerful will to achieve political unity. The unification of the Italian States which took place at almost the same period, from 1859 to 1870, exemplifies the perils which a widened market may bring to certain regions when, in addition to differences in the type of economic activity of the various regions, and in their economic outlook, there are also real and profound disparities in the stages of economic development which they have reached.

The economies of the States of southern Italy were based almost entirely upon agriculture and a few craft industries. The States of the north, on the other hand, although they also had a substantial if more prosperous agriculture, were in a stage of rapid industrial development; communications were easier and capital was more plentiful. According to the rules of liberal economic theory the expansion of the market by the union of north and south should have given the southern States full scope for economic progress; but this did not happen. The mechanisms which should have attracted capital and investments to the low-wage economy of the south did not function. Instead of the expected classic process of a restoration of balance, there was a concentration of activity in the already prosperous regions. The weak industries of the south were almost entirely wiped out, whilst those of the north benefited from the widened market. Instead of providing a magnet for investment, the over-abundant labour force of the south moved north in search of work. Similarly, southern capital, instead of being invested locally, went to swell the investments in the north, where industry was thriving and quicker profits could be earned; thus the disparity between the two regions was increased still further.

THE 'COLONIAL' EMPIRES

During the nineteenth century a number of industrial countries benefited from a different kind of expansion of markets; the conquest, by England and France in particular, of so-called 'colonial' markets. It is undoubtedly true that the existence of the Commonwealth is one of the factors making for English industrial strength; imperial preferences go a long way towards reserving an enormous market for British industry. But cases of this kind are extremely complex; the links which actually bind the Commonwealth together tend increasingly to be purely monetary. Moreover, the relationship between Great Britain and its Commonwealth, like that of France and the French Union, is characterised by a whole series of complex benefits and counter-benefits, price-supports and guaranteed purchases, mutual advantages and disadvantages, which have made it possible to keep trade in balance. But it is doubtful whether this unity can be maintained unless the mother countries can look beyond the mere size of the markets available to them and adopt a policy of investing in the development of every area, even when there is no financial return. The unification of markets always gives rise to the same political problems of initiative, authority and balance, but since the war, in particular, the need for a new economic balance has become apparent.

As we pointed out in the introduction, it was during the Second World War that the vital need became apparent for closer co-operation – both economic and political – between the countries of Europe. The first fruit of this idea was an attempt to establish customs unions between countries which were closely linked by history and geography.

BENELUX

The basic decision to establish the so-called 'Benelux' customs union between Belgium, the Netherlands and Luxembourg was taken as long ago as 1943, and the first conventions were signed in 1943 and 1944. It was agreed, however, that the customs union should not come into force until the financial, economic and social policies of the three countries had been co-ordinated to a certain extent and until the effects of that co-ordination had begun to make themselves felt. As from 1948 all customs duties were abolished between the Belgian-Luxembourg Economic Union on the one hand and the Netherlands on the other hand, and a common tariff was instituted for foreign goods. In 1949 an agreement for 'preliminary union' established a plan for the progressive abolition of quantitative restrictions. This cautious and empirical approach can be explained by the initial disparities between the economies of the two countries; it can also be considered as one of the factors making for the success of the operation. Average wages in Belgium were 60% above those of Holland. Belgian agriculture was less developed and less attuned to export, whereas Belgian industry appeared to be stronger than that of Holland. There was also a great difference in the post-war economic policies of the two countries, the Netherlands having followed a policy of austerity and rigorous price-control.

The experience gained over a number of years would seem to indicate that these disparities have not prevented a substantial increase in trade between the two countries and a more or less equal participation by the two countries in that increase. Belgian sales to the Netherlands, which formed eight per cent of the latter country's imports in 1948, increased to 13% in 1956. Purchases by the Netherlands from Belgium rose from 12% in 1948 to 22% in 1956. In absolute figures Belgium tripled its sales to and purchases from Holland between 1948 and 1956. These results were achieved without any grave repercussions, and the only occasion on which it proved necessary to invoke the escape clauses was after the Korean War, when prices rose much more quickly in Belgium than in Holland. On the contrary, it appears that a considerable number of specialisation agreements between industries in the two countries have enabled both countries to expand their industrial activity. Simultaneously, wage levels and economic policies in the two countries have been brought closer together. Although wages are still higher in Belgium the discrepancy is now only 38%. Contrary to expectation, there has been no sign of one country specialising solely in agriculture and the other in industry; production conditions in Belgian agriculture are tending to draw nearer to those of Dutch agriculture, while Dutch industry has been diversified and has grown considerably stronger. In short, it would appear that the two countries have benefited from their economic merger, even though the benefits may not have been exactly equal. Nevertheless, as far as agriculture is concerned, the progress made in the application of the Treaty has not been as substantial as might have been expected.

THE FRANCO-ITALIAN PROJECT

A Franco-Italian customs union was the subject of similar negotiations from 1947 onwards. A Treaty was signed in Paris in 1949, but was soon abandoned as it became evident that the advantages of a mere expansion of the market between the two countries were considerably outweighed by the serious difficulties to which it gave rise. The two economies frequently proved to be competitive, particularly in agriculture. The inherent advantages of a large market could not produce appreciable advantages except in a wider context. It was at one time thought that this venture might be incorporated with Benelux, under the picturesque title of 'Fritalux', thus approaching in scope the future Europe of the Common Market. But at this juncture, the prospect opened up by the O.E.E.C. was destined to direct attention towards another type of co-operation.

THE O.E.E.C.

The Organisation for European Economic Co-operation followed these commercial lines while deliberately rejecting the bilateralism which had characterised European trade in the troubled pre-war years and the immediate post-war years. In his speech at Harvard on June 5th 1947, General Marshall had stated that American aid to Europe, if it was to be effective must be accompanied by a much closer economic co-operation between the countries of Europe, and the first task of the O.E.E.C. was not merely to distribute the foreign aid but also to work out a rational development plan for the European economies. Its work in co-ordinating economic and social policies has been limited, however, by its intergovernmental structure and the requirement of unanimity in its procedure, and also by the profound differences in the conditions prevailing among the seventeen participating countries, which range from England to Turkey and from Sweden to Portugal. In the strictly commercial field, however, the O.E.E.C. has played a most useful part in promoting a progressive multilateral easing of the system of import quotas.

The European Payments Union, which was established in July 1950, considerably eased this work of increasing trade by providing for multilateral financial clearings, including the grant of credit to debtor countries. But as it only dealt with the problems of quantitative trade restrictions, and in the monetary field it only provided for clearing arrangements or extended payments, without touching the fundamental causes of disequilibrium, the O.E.E.C. found its activities severely circumscribed. As soon as the freeing of imports began to reach a high level, or when particularly sensitive sectors were affected, negotiations became increasingly difficult and other very delicate problems arose which had to be solved in order to achieve an overall balance and which thus determined every step forward in the actual field of quotas: disparity in the levels of customs duties, the need to maintain a balance between agriculture and industry, possibilities for the movement of capital or labour, co-ordination of economic policies, etc.; progress slowed down; in fact, cases occurred where a particular country found itself in economic or monetary difficulties and it was even necessary to go back on engagements which had been made previously. Hence it seemed essential to embark on the creation of a larger market which was not purely commercial in character and which provided, at least in one sector, an economic integration in depth.

THE E.C.S.C.

The Treaty which set up the European Coal and Steel Community (E.C.S.C.) provides an example of a pooling of resources and markets in a limited sphere under the control of a specialised authority. In this respect the E.C.S.C. can be regarded as a sort of proving ground for the wider Common Market. The Treaty was signed in 1951 by France, Germany, Italy and the three Benelux countries, and it came into force in 1952. It does more than liberalise trade, and it is a binding contract. Precisely because the effective conditions of an economic integration are to be achieved, a system of independent institutions has to be established, to provide the necessary driving force and to ensure that the Treaty is exactly applied. This system comprises an executive body, a court of justice and a parliamentary assembly. Thus it is a European government in embryo, intended to have a policy of its own as well as to co-ordinate the policies of the participating countries. In effect, the application of the Treaty does not merely involve a reduction of tariff barriers and a progressive abolition of bilateral or multilateral quota systems. The goal is a balanced market and a balanced production. A certain number of rules for competition have to be laid down and respected in order to ensure that the widened markets benefit all consumers and conform fully with economic progress. A labour policy has also to be worked out to facilitate the necessary retraining and resettlement. Finally, in this vital sector of basic industry, a concerted and effective investment policy is essential.

In assessing the results of the E.C.S.C. it is not easy to disentangle those which arise out of the Treaty and the work of its institutions from those which are due to general economic trends; nevertheless this restricted Community seems to show an unmistakable balance on the credit side, in spite of certain deficiencies. Production has gone up, increasing in the case of steel from 40 to 70 million tons per annum, and the increase has been markedly greater in the countries of the Community, and their products, than in the remainder of Europe. Trade has increased three times more rapidly than production, contrary to the experience of previous boom periods. Secondly, as regards the structure of the industries, the necessary work of modernisation has been carried out with the aid of the Community's funds, whilst subsidies from national funds have been steadily reduced. 200 million dollars have been raised for investment through the agency of the High Authority. Finally, in the social field, fifty thousand workers in France, Belgium and Italy have benefited from measures of retraining and resettlement; wage levels and working conditions in the six countries have undoubtedly tended to draw together and in an upward direction.

Although all the countries of the E.C.S.C. have enjoyed an increase in trade it is not certain that all of them have benefited equally. The country which was probably the last to develop industrially, Italy, has certainly come out relatively better than any of the others. There has been no major revival of the French economy as some people may have hoped, but France has gained many technical benefits, including, in particular, regular supplies of Ruhr coke. Her sales of steel to the other countries of the E.C.S.C. have increased fourfold. The cost of transporting a ton of coke from the Ruhr to Lorraine has decreased by 30%. Moreover, it is certain that the merging of markets, whether as an inducement or a potential threat, has stimulated efforts towards modernisation, rationalisation and specialisation in industry. On the other hand, there has been a serious coal crisis since 1958, principally in Belgium; this crisis is due partly to conditions peculiar to Belgian production, but more particularly to a basic shift in fuel utilization throughout the world. Thus, from 1950 to 1960, the proportion of the energy requirements of the Community covered by coal dropped from 72·5% to 53·8%. From 1957 to 1959 alone, coal consumption went down by 16% (whilst production decreased by only 5%) mainly to the advantage of fuel oil and natural gas. Various measures have been taken with regard to stockpiling, closure of pits, unemployment relief, and imports of foreign coal. But the problem is a long-term one which calls for a truly integrated fuel policy.

On these, as on other grounds, it is to be regretted that the E.C.S.C. has not played a more active co-ordinating role. Great caution seems to have been displayed on all sides in approaching problems which were clearly political rather than technical. And the freedom of action of the High Authority has been hampered by the fact that its powers are restricted to one particular sector; this is the case particularly in regard to economic policy, prices, investment, etc.

Attempts have been made to extend the coal and steel experiment to other fields. The earliest attempt was the French proposal for a 'green pool', or integration of agriculture. The countries which took part in the negotiations were agreed on certain aims: the need for a balanced European agriculture, an efficient organisation of markets and a very gradual implementation of any proposals; but divergencies became apparent over the economic policies to be followed and over the list of products to be included. A contributory cause of the failure of the project was the particular opposition of Great Britain, which constitutes the largest European agricultural market but is linked by its imperial preference agreements with an agricultural trading area outside Europe. Other projects for specialised 'pools' followed, but on none of them has agreement been reached.

It appears that economic integration restricted to one field has a reasonably good chance of succeeding if that field is sufficiently clearly defined to permit efficient technical co-ordination without affecting the general policies of each participating country. If the field is less clearly defined, or wider, it quickly becomes impossible to contemplate its integration in isolation, and the general policies of each country must be affected. In any event, within a single sector it is very difficult to overcome the conflicts of interest between the various countries. Hence the principal virtue of the formula of integration by sectors is that it provides an experimental approach and also that it almost inevitably sets in motion a pooling of markets and resources on a much wider scale. Only in such a framework can the conflicting individual interests be subjected to a process of give and take at the negotiating stage, and the mechanisms of general readjustment and counter-balance between the different sectors be given a chance to operate when it comes to applying the agreement. The risks are undoubtedly greater, but there is much more likelihood of helping the economies of the participating countries.

This complete pooling of resources and outlets raises another problem, however: that of the *geographical area* over which it is to be applied. In the case of an agreement in a limited technical sphere, the inclusion of a large number of countries can be envisaged; but it is very difficult to bring into a completely integrated economy with all the obligations which that integration inevitably entails, countries which are too widely separated in their geography, history and economic and social structure. Thus, from the point of view of the number of participants and the size of the Common Market, a certain 'optimum' or mean emerges between the advantages of widening its scope and the actual possibilities of putting it into operation.

CHAPTER III

The Economics of Large Markets

IF we study the experiments which have already been made we can pick out a certain number of economic laws governing large markets, which fall into two categories: negative and positive. It would seem that the incompatibilities or dangers which are often forecast do not in fact arise. On the other hand certain mechanisms of re-adjustment which have been taken for granted also tend not to function in the present state of economic and social development. Hence the operation of large markets, while disposing of certain theoretical objections, involves the adoption of an active policy of adjustment and balancing simultaneously with the freeing of trade.

THE TOTAL WAGE BILL

'Wage levels' must be understood to cover not only direct wages, but also all the additional welfare payments which go with wages to form much the largest element in production costs. There are two possible ways of approaching this problem. One is the global approach of comparing the average level of wages in one country with that prevailing in competitor countries; the other is the specific approach which involves a study of the amount and incidence of wages sector by sector or even firm by firm, according to the countries concerned.

As regards the global approach, it is not easy to make exact comparisons of wage and price levels in various countries owing to the varied patterns of consumption, the complex structure of the wage bill and the variations in its incidence. In some countries a part of the welfare charges are 'budgetised' and paid out of taxation, whilst in other countries the whole wage bill is met directly by industry; there is also the fact that in some countries, such as Germany, the range of optional contributions is at least as great as that of the statutory contributions which play a much bigger role in France. Further, owing to the lack of an international monetary standard, or of a freedom which would allow the various currencies to find their own levels in accordance with their purchasing power, the present frequently artificial exchange rates tend to distort comparisons. Nevertheless, it is quite true that there are very considerable differences in wage level as between one European country and another, differences which may exceed 50% in the case of the Mediterranean and Scandinavian countries for instance. Such marked differences, which are automatically reflected in production costs, would rule out the possibility of competition based on a complete abolition of customs duties and other protective mechanisms.

This problem can be considered from two standpoints: that of theory and that of actual experience. The general level of wages and social charges is in fact only a reflection of differences in productivity. In theory, rates of exchange tend to adapt themselves to the levels of prices and costs, so that each country will have its fair share of production and exports, and a certain international division of labour will be maintained. High wages may appear to be a disadvantage in international competition, but they may also be regarded merely as the consequence of a thriving economy. It is only when high wages are not the logical outcome of a strong economy and high productivity that they give rise to imbalance in international trade. But in such a case it is clear that this imbalance cannot continue; a new equilibrium must be established, either by the operation of the rate of exchange or as a result of a more restrictive or selective internal policy. This point is brought out in a report of the experts of the International Labour Office in Geneva:

> 'As long as there continue to be differences in productivity, disparities in the general level of workers' wages as between one country and another, far from being an obstacle to a liberalisation of international trade, will be essential in order that production and incomes in all the participating countries may be as high as possible.'

Turning from theory to fact it again appears that differences in the general price level do not rule out the possibility of competition, in spite of the fears which have always been expressed on this point. In the Benelux union the average level of Belgian wages in 1947 was 60% above that of Dutch wages, yet this marked disparity did not prevent Belgium from tripling its sales to Holland between 1948 and 1956.

SPECIFIC DISTORTIONS

But the outlook is more uncertain if the differences in wages, and hence in production costs, are examined sector by sector and found to be due to disparities in development in a certain sector as between one country and another; the problem is more serious when the differences are due to divergences in social and fiscal legislation. It is difficult to see how, within a particular sector or industry, a readjustment mechanism can operate to improve its competitive power.

This is the case, for instance, when the labour force in a particular sector is by tradition predominantly feminine and when equal pay for women is enforced by law in a particular country but not in the competing country, where women's wages may be 40% below men's. When the market is widened, specific distortions of this kind would very probably cause difficulties, and if wage rates cannot be brought into line it would seem necessary to provide for safeguards in the most patent cases.

THE PROBLEM OF SECURING A NEW ECONOMIC EQUILIBRIUM

The problem of differing price levels can, as we have seen, be reduced to one of specific distortions, but the economics of large markets have brought to light other problems for which a solution must be found. In the first place, the play of adjustment mechanisms assumes not only the possibility of price adjustments by means of alterations in rates of exchange but also the possibility that economic activity as a whole may be brought into a new equilibrium by the free movement of capital and labour. But in the world of today this freedom of movement is either largely theoretical or else more dangerous than desirable. To depend entirely on the possibility of a mass migration of labour to counter-balance the increase of wages in areas of over-employment would be to under-estimate the reluctance of workers to move in large numbers and the reluctance of those in charge of social policy to receive them. Similarly, it is not possible to rely on the free movement of capital as a means of ensuring a better economic balance in investment while ignoring the fact that in the less-developed regions the relatively lower wage level does not provide an adequate incentive for investment; account must be taken of the established patterns of investment which favour the existing concentrations, and of the dangers inherent in violent movements based on speculative or psychological considerations.

The problem can be posed in these terms: if the various regions or countries which would be brought together by the pooling of markets have much the same levels of economic and social development and financial resources, then there will be no grave disparities in their competitive power; moreover the mechanisms of readjustment in the form of movements of capital and labour, can come into play to the advantage of all the members. On the other hand, when the degree of disparity between the countries or regions concerned is so great as to constitute virtually a difference in the nature of their standards of living and economic strength, then the expansion of the market and the liberal principles of free competition and better division of labour and capital may not result in a restoration of the balance between the various countries; in fact they may even seriously widen the initial disparities.

A case in point is the unification of the Italian market in the nineteenth century, which was mentioned in the last chapter. The same problem would arise in our day if an attempt was made to turn the whole of Europe into a single market without any advance preparations and without any adjustment mechanism. Even among the six countries of the E.C.S.C., although they have much in common, it was considered necessary to provide adjustment mechanisms of very wide scope in order to allow all countries to reach a level of economic development which would give them all equal opportunities.

From these observations we can draw two general conclusions as to the possibilities of achieving an overall equilibrium.

A pooling of markets is dangerous if it merely consists in pooling the domestic difficulties of all the states concerned. If the expansion of the market is to lead towards the establishment of an equilibrium there must be reserves of flexibility and plenty of room for manoeuvre; there must be opportunities for each economy to specialise within the enlarged market or, failing that, there must be an assurance of a serious effort to develop the less-favoured regions. The unification of Italy and France on their own would merely tend to aggravate the imbalance and the surpluses of both countries, but within the framework of a larger unification both Italy and France will have the fullest opportunities of development (this extension of the geographical area is itself circumscribed, as has been mentioned above, by the political and practical feasibility of setting states on the road towards integration). It is not necessary, however, that the various economies should be exactly complementary; the example of Benelux has shown the unreality of such fears when the economy as a whole is expanding. It is a fact that industrial countries have always been the best customers of industrial countries.

A further necessary condition is that the economies which are to be pooled shall be pooled completely. A large market can only succeed if it covers a reasonably wide area and also has sufficient depth to allow of considerable readjustment. The free movement of goods, on its own, may bring some limited benefits, but it is liable to cause serious harm to certain sectors of the economy. When, however, it is accompanied by a movement towards alignment in all the ancillary spheres of currency, finance and social policy, it can further the economic development of all the participants.

However, even when the economy as a whole is developing, the development may not be uniform. The widening of the market in the United States, as in Italy or Germany, caused an undeniable increase in the average standards of living, but some regions, countries or sectors certainly obtained more benefit from this development than others. The problem is to ascertain to what extent these variations in the pace and intensity of economic development are healthy from the point of view of productivity and to what extent they are tolerable from the human and political angle. At the time when railways were being built in France the lines were deliberately planned so as not to deprive any region of the possibility of development, regardless of the very high cost of railways in the poorer regions and the low profit they would yield. In post-war Italy the establishment of a special finance organisation to develop the southern regions betokens the same political anxiety, to offset (by artificial means where necessary) the disparity in the economic development of the regions.

In a Common Market which has been widened to include several countries exactly the same question arises. Granted that the large market will confer some benefits on everyone, some means must still be found of ensuring that the disparity between those benefits is not too great. Consideration must then be given to the incorporation in the expanded market of adjustment mechanisms which will work towards a harmonious development of the newly created economic unit.

THE ROLE OF COMPETITION

So far we have only considered the possibilities of an overall equilibrium between countries within the framework of a Common Market. But a widening of the market on this scale may also have direct consequences, inside each country, on the relations between individual firms and on the structure of each firm considered in isolation. The object of widening the market is to raise standards of living and enable consumers to buy more easily and at lower prices; the new facilities of specialisation, mass production, etc., which are available to producers, are only means to achieve that end. It is by no means certain, however, that this end will be achieved automatically as a result of the advantages granted to industry, unless the door is closed to certain practices which are liable to distort the free play of competition.

It is true that in a large market it is much more difficult for a single firm to obtain complete control of the market and thus achieve its aim of establishing monopoly prices. For firms with huge resources, however, the stakes probably justify a supreme effort. In particular, unless the movements of capital and investments are controlled, a large market is a strong temptation to firms, either inside or outside the Common Market, to make a powerful and sustained attempt to obtain control of the enlarged market.

But in practice the main tendency is likely to be towards agreements between firms.

Where such agreements are backed up by the necessary specialisation and lead to substantial reductions in selling prices, they are in harmony with the objectives of the large market. But where they merely involve a division of markets without any benefit for the consumer they can wipe out a great part of the advantages which a common market should bring. There undoubtedly is a tendency towards action of this kind, as is evident from the example of the United States and, on a smaller scale, that of the E.C.S.C. On the other hand it is extremely difficult to know whether this is a healthy tendency and to what extent it can be controlled and channelled for the benefit of the community as a whole. The difficulties of applying decartellisation in Germany and anti-trust legislation in America are well known. Nevertheless it is particularly important in a large market that certain rules of competition should be laid down and observed.

SMALL BUSINESSES

Turning to the internal structure of firms, it may appear that a large market is an *a priori* incentive to big business, and that the working of competition or of restrictive agreements may tend to wipe out the smaller producers. But the example of the United States shows that, in spite of the role played by a few spectacular 'giants' such as General Motors, General Electric, United Fruit and Standard Oil, the picture is by no means clear-cut and there are opportunities for small firms as well as large ones.

General Motors, for instance, works with 21,000 sub-contractors; 42,000 sub-contractors, 90% of them small firms, contribute to General Electric's sales figures. Since 1946 the total number of businesses in America, far from diminishing, has increased by nine per cent, and 75% of all American firms employ less than four workers. In sectors like building, commerce and services, the large firms only employ one per cent of the labour force. As regards results, it may be mentioned that the share of profits obtained by the smaller firms rose from 20% in 1929 to more than 32% in 1948.

Hence it would seem that in a very large market the small firms can hold their own perfectly well in many sectors, and that the specialisation made possible by increased sales outlets favours the survival and prosperity of very small units. Moreover, general economic progress, even when it leads to the establishment of big businesses or widespread agreements between firms, inevitably brings more work to a very large number of vendors and sub-contractors. Nevertheless, a general rule can be laid down similar to that which applies to equilibria between one state and another: although all firms, irrespective of their size, will inevitably benefit from the expansion of the market they will not all benefit in exactly the same proportion. There are some sectors, particularly the converting industries, where the big firms seem to be in a stronger position. On the other hand, although the small firms stand to benefit substantially from the general economic expansion in a large market, they will be the first to suffer if boom gives place to slump.

EFFECTS ON THE ECONOMIC CYCLE

The large market affects not only the balance of one economy or one firm in relation to another at a given moment, but also, in due course, the general cycles of activity. From the point of view of continuity of economic growth, which takes the form of alternating phases of expansion and recession, the large market appears to contribute a new element of stability. Instead of taking their cue more or less blindly from the most transient symptoms of the economic situation, and thus running the risk of setting in motion chain reactions which can soon get out of hand, a number of influential firms have a definite policy which is better informed and above all is worked out over a longer period. They have a better appreciation of the role played by wages in the economy.

With the assurance of bigger markets, investments are better planned, on a longer-term basis, and are carried out more rationally and steadily. In the field of sales policy there is a tendency to abandon direct competition with other firms and price-cutting campaigns with their violent repercussions on consumption; efforts are concentrated instead on an expansion of the market as a whole by means of research, improved quality and education of public taste.

The history of the American market in recent years, for instance, reveals that fluctuations in economic activity due to recurrent depressions have become much less severe. During the depression of 1929 total production dropped by 30%, whereas in the recessions of 1948 and 1953 the drop was less than two per cent in each case. Thanks, therefore, to the leading role which big firms are destined to play in it, the large market helps to provide more possibilities of forecasting economic changes, of spreading out uncontrollable variations and, finally, ensuring some stability of expansion. As small firms can benefit directly from the large market by a certain degree of specialisation, and as it is they who have the most to fear from fluctuations, it would seem that an enlargement of the market makes a significant contribution, if not to the preservation of the existing economic structure, at least to the steadying of economic activity, to the advantage of the community as a whole.

But this optimism, the fruit of experience, must be qualified by the following observation. Although a large market provides a framework for a stable expansion, the smaller markets also manifested a certain stability which was inherent in a limited and cautious economy. Whereas the crisis of 1929 caused a great upheaval in the American economy, its effects were cushioned in the divided economy of Europe and particularly in France. It would appear that a strong economy, based on a large market, has much greater powers of resistance in the face of a crisis, but that when the disturbance has reached a certain intensity various cumulative processes are set in violent motion and the repercussions are much graver.

But this is a criticism which can be levelled against any economic expansion, since all expansion is to some extent a permanent gamble on the future with continually increasing stakes. And the existence of a large unified market cannot but reduce the odds on this gamble while retaining its advantages.

PART II

The Common Market Treaty

CHAPTER IV

Definition of the Common Market

In June 1955 the Foreign Ministers of the six member countries of the European Coal and Steel Community met at Messina and decided, on the basis of a memorandum from Benelux, to re-launch the European idea in the economic field. The final communiqué stated:

> 'The development of a united Europe must be pursued by the development of common institutions, the progressive fusion of national economies, the creation of a common market and the progressive harmonization of their social policies.'

As we emphasized at the outset, this was the convergence of an economic trend toward freer trade and a political trend towards European unification, centred round the idea of a Common Market of six countries freed from all tariff and quota restrictions.

But the lines on which this idea was to be put into practice had still to be worked out. The six ministers decided that before the Common Market could be brought into existence a certain number of questions would have to be studied:

> The procedure and the pace to be adopted for the progressive abolition of trade barriers, as well as the

appropriate measures for moving towards a progressive unification of their tariffs against third countries.[1]

The harmonization of the general policies of the participating countries in the financial, economic and social fields.

The co-ordination of monetary policies in so far as this may appear necessary.

The setting up of a fund for readaptation, and the progressive introduction of free movement of labour.

The establishment of rules of competition, particularly with a view to preventing discrimination on grounds of nationality.

The establishment of an investment fund to develop the less favoured regions of the participating States.

The progressive harmonization of legislation operating in the social field, particularly in regard to hours of work.

This list of questions which were to be solved before any negotiations began provides some extremely interesting pointers to the principles and practices of a Common Market as it might be conceived in the light of theory and of historical experience. At the same time a negotiating procedure had been worked out. It was to be based on a preliminary report by a committee of governmental representatives under the chairmanship of a leading political personality, M. Spaak.

THE SPAAK REPORT

The work took a considerable time and encountered considerable difficulties, but it produced extremely useful

[1] Third countries: see note on page 57.

results. It was not until April 1956 that the heads of delegations were able to hand this preliminary report to their ministers. But when they met at Venice in May 1956 the six ministers of foreign affairs were able to adopt the report in its entirety as a draft for the future treaty.

The experts' report, often called *The Spaak Report*, laid down a certain number of principles:

> The object of a European Common Market should be to create a vast area with a common political economy which will form a powerful productive unit and permit a steady expansion, an increase in stability, a more rapid rise in the standard of living, and the development of harmonious relations between the Member States.
>
> .... But the advantages of a Common Market (in the technical field of production) can only be secured if there is flexibility in the timetable and if means are provided collectively to permit the necessary adjustments, if the distortion of competition between producers is abolished, and if the States co-operate to ensure monetary stability, economic expansion and social progress. This is the basic reason why a true Common Market can only be established between a certain optimum number of States, however desirable a world-wide system of free trade might appear in theory. A Common Market can only be regional, *i.e.*, between States which feel themselves sufficiently close to each other to be able to make the necessary legislative adjustments and to enforce the necessary solidarity in their policies.

After outlining the Common Market in broad terms the authors of the report drew certain conclusions concerning the institutions required to achieve the chosen objectives. They made a distinction between a permanent, independent body, the 'European Commission', which could make rapid decisions on technical questions and generally supply the initiative, and a body representing the Member States, the 'Council of Ministers', which would make decisions in accordance with very flexible majority voting systems suited to the various fields of action and the various stages of implementation of the treaty. The division of powers between these two organs would be supplemented by the double check of a Court of Justice and an Assembly.

THE BRUSSELS NEGOTIATIONS

The report was already a compromise. From the start some opposition had been apparent between a liberal wing, which aimed merely to abolish existing trade barriers in the shortest possible time, and a group of countries such as France which were more apprehensive of the effects of such a strictly liberal trade policy. There had been a gradual realisation of the fact that the full participation of the six countries could only be secured if the scope of the Treaty was extended to non-commercial matters, if plenty of time was allowed for its implementation, and if a sufficiently high external customs tariff was provided. Nevertheless, the Brussels report was still somewhat vague on certain points, and no solution was provided to some extremely delicate problems such as agriculture, the harmonization of social charges and the association of overseas territories. Negotiations in the full sense of the word were therefore taken up by the experts of the six countries in June 1956, working on the basis of the *Spaak Report*. For nearly two years the centre of negotiations moved backwards and forwards between the experts working at Val-Duchesse, a secluded Belgian crown estate in the forest outside Brussels, and the heads of government who met in the capital cities when a compromise could only be found or ratified at the highest political level.

An original solution was worked out at Brussels for the problem of increasing trade in agricultural products, within the framework of a common agricultural policy. In regard to the harmonization of social charges the initial projects of the experts were supplemented by clarifications and guarantees as the result of a meeting between the French and German heads of government in November 1956. Similarly, in regard to the phasing of the measures for the removal of protective tariffs and quotas, a special institutional procedure was devised which gave additional flexibility at the decisive transition from the first to the second stage. As to the association of overseas territories with the European Common Market, an idea which France had first put forward at the time of the Venice Conference, it was again at a top-level meeting of heads of government at Paris in February 1957 that an agreement was reached, setting out both the general objectives and the provisional procedure for their implementation.

Finally, many of the technical provisions for the establishment of the Common Market were dealt with by clarifying or substantially adding to the Brussels report. The general trend was towards a pooling of markets and resources, but with a balance in the provisions of the Treaty as a whole to temper it to the needs of the less thriving economies; there was also a trend towards the establishment of a balance in the institutions, giving considerable powers to the organs of the Community to deal with the particular problems which could not fail to arise when the Treaty came to be applied.

The Treaty signed in Rome on 25th March 1957 between Germany, France, Italy, the Netherlands, Belgium and Luxembourg, is generally known as the Common Market, but its official title is the more appropriate one of European Economic Community. The Treaty is not a mere trade agreement to facilitate exports and imports; the aim is in fact to establish a true economic community between the six countries concerned. This will be brought out more clearly by an examination of the provisions of the Treaty in later chapters.

The *Spaak Report* and the Val-Duchesse negotiations showed that the advantages of an expansion of the market were not by themselves sufficient to dispel all fears or to offset all the possible adverse effects of adjustment on all the partners. The originality of the Treaty lies in the fact that it attempts to ensure a harmonious working of the Common Market, leading towards a complete fusion of the various national markets, by bringing the economic and social systems of the countries sufficiently close together to ensure fair competition and equitable possibilities of development. Hence the Common Market Treaty – or more correctly the Treaty of the European Economic Community – goes beyond the mere mechanisms of trade and provides for the achievement of a necessary minimum of economic integration, under the control of appropriate institutions, to go hand in hand with the progressive freeing of the movement of goods.

THE TREATY IN OUTLINE

The basis and the prime purpose of the Treaty, however, is the abolition of trade barriers, tariffs and quotas. The other provisions all hinge upon this process, which in fact is the actual process by which the market is established. The abolition is to be completed more or less automatically in a period of from twelve to fifteen years. This transition period, as it is called, is itself divided into three stages, each designed to last for four years. A series of targets are assigned to each stage, under the supervision of the institutions of the community, and these targets are related not only to progress in the removal of trade barriers but also to the parallel measures of economic and social alignment.

The abolition of customs duties and quantitative restrictions as between member States is to be accompanied by the establishment, at a similar pace, of a common external tariff *vis-à-vis* third countries[1]; this entitles the Treaty of Rome to be considered juridically as a customs union, as distinct from a free trade area, and it forms the major element of unification within the Community. Moreover, inside this unified tariff wall the alignment of the economies is to be carried out by means of internal mechanisms to adjust the differences in price, working conditions, and distribution of productive resources. These mechanisms comprise a harmonization of social policies, an effective procedure for correcting distortions in competitive conditions, a common

[1] The expression 'third country, third countries' refers to countries outside the Common Market, as being outside the dialogue between members of the Common Market.

agricultural policy to bring prices into alignment, a co-ordination of monetary policies, mutual assistance in case of balance of payments difficulties, a social fund and a European bank, and finally the germ of a system for sharing the burdens of assistance to under-developed countries.

To ensure a simultaneous development of the Common Market and of the common economic and social policy which are to be associated with it, the operation of more or less automatic machinery for the reduction of customs barriers has been linked to a confirmation[1] of the progress achieved in the other fields of the Treaty. This link is provided by the procedure for transition from the first to the second stage of the expansion of the market. It is at this stage that further steps towards a free market will be made conditional upon the confirmation of effective progress on certain items which are indispensable to the satisfactory functioning of the market, in particular the development of trade in agricultural products by means of long-term agreements, the equalisation of pay for men and women, and the establishment of a common external tariff.

Thus the stages of the transition period reflect not merely a desire to move a step at a time towards the achievement of the Common Market, and so permit the necessary adjustments, but also a will to achieve unity, which is in keeping with the wide scope of the Treaty and with the need to maintain a balance all the time in its application.

But the Treaty of Rome does not attempt to establish a political community, and the machinery of co-ordination is restricted to the minimum requirements which

[1]The 'confirmation' (or 'confirmatory statement') is explained on page 100.

can be foreseen at present or, to use the definition which appears on numerous occasions, 'so far as necessary to the proper working of the Common Market'. To go any further would involve a serious encroachment on the essential preserves of the political independence of the member States; it would also immediately raise useless arguments on economic theory. Many people will regard this as a defect, but possibly one of the great virtues of the Treaty is that it keeps as far as possible from the doctrinal disputes between supporters of a liberal and a managed economy, putting its trust in the procedures which the Treaty prescribes should experience show that decisions in one direction or another have become necessary. What is important is the certainty that the decisions can be taken.

THE ULTIMATE OBJECTIVE

It is important to realize that this caution, which is inevitable in view of the instability of economic conditions, reflects a vital but often unrecognized objective: that of ensuring that the Treaty is applied *in toto* and its aims fully achieved; this was very much in the minds of the negotiators and is one of the distinctive features of the Common Market.

It is relatively easy to *begin* to reduce trade barriers between States, but it is difficult to continue beyond the first steps. It is even more difficult to complete the process, to create a new unit in which all the barriers have been completely removed. This has been proved by other experiments. The economic success of the Common Market (and the potentialities for political development which form one of the reasons for its existence) are determined not by the start of the operations but by the possibility of carrying them to a final and successful conclusion. It is at this final stage, and only then, that the greatest technical, economic and political benefits will become evident.

It is in this light that we must regard many of the provisions of the Treaty and the framework of the Treaty as a whole: the determination to achieve a balance between the different sectors and between the various types of obligation, the desire for steady development and flexibility, and finally, perhaps most important of all, the creation of independent institutions, vested with powers of their own and able to guide and lead at all times.

CHAPTER V

The Free Movement of Goods within the Customs Union

> The Community shall be based upon a customs union covering the exchange of all goods and comprising both the prohibition, as between Member States, of customs duties on importation and exportation, and all charges with equivalent effect, and the adoption of a common customs tariff in their relations with third countries.

As a parallel measure the Treaty provides for the abolition as between Member States of all quantitative restrictions on imports and exports. The free movement of goods within the Community applies not only to products originating in the Member States but also to products imported from third countries on which customs duties and charges of equivalent effect have been paid on entry into one of the Member States; these products are then said to be 'in free practice' within the Community. The establishment of a common customs tariff and the extension of freedom of movement to products in free practice form two of the essential characteristics of a customs union. In a free trade area, on the other hand, each Member State retains its own tariffs against third countries at the level which it deems fit, and products originating in third countries cannot circulate freely within the area.

CUSTOMS DUTIES

Customs duties on imports and exports between Member States are to have been completely abolished by the end of the transition period of twelve to fifteen years at the latest. Taking as a base the duties in force on 1 January 1957, a first reduction of ten per cent was applied uniformly to all duties one year after the Treaty came into force (1 January 1959). During the first stage two other reductions of ten per cent are to be made at intervals of eighteen months. During the second stage two reductions of ten per cent will be made at intervals of eighteen months and a third reduction at the end of the second stage. At this point the timing of the final reductions will be decided by the Council of Ministers, acting by means of a qualified majority.[1]

If all existing duties were to be reduced by the same percentage there would be no possibility of making exceptions. The method adopted is more flexible and leaves a certain freedom of choice to each government: the first reduction of ten per cent is applied uniformly, but in the case of the subsequent reductions some duties may be cut by only five per cent, provided that the duties as a whole are still reduced by ten per cent. Thus half the burden of reduction can be allocated by each government at its discretion in the light of the needs of home industries. Governments must, however, endeavour

[1]The term 'qualified majority' is explained on page 97.

to ensure that the reduction on each individual product reaches at least 25% by the end of the first stage and 50% by the end of the second stage.

Customs duties or taxes on exports are to be abolished not later than the end of the first stage. Customs duties of a fiscal nature, which are applied to certain consumer goods for budgetary purposes only, are subject in principle to the rules for the abolition of customs duties as between Member States. Nevertheless, the Member States retain the right to replace these duties by internal taxes applied without discrimination to home and imported products.

QUANTITATIVE RESTRICTIONS (QUOTAS)

Simultaneously with the elimination of customs duties, the abolition of all quantitative restrictions on trade between Member States is to be effected by the end of the transition period, at the latest. The procedure adopted differs from that used in O.E.E.C. in that it is based not on the abolition of the entire quota on each product, one at a time, but on a progressive increase in existing quotas which makes them less and less effective as protectionist implements until, by the end of the transition period they can be abolished quite naturally. Moreover, the first step towards unification of the market under the terms of the Treaty is to be the ending of bilateralism between the Member States: one year after the Treaty comes into force all bilateral quotas granted by each State are to be transformed into global quotas in which all the other Member States can share on an equal footing. This global quota is then to be increased by at least 20% each year. Governments do, however, retain a certain field of manoeuvre, since this minimum increase of 20% can be spread over different products in varying degree, provided that the global quota for each product is increased by not less than ten per cent yearly.

The system of percentage increases would not allow of any effective liberalisation of the market when the basic quota is nil or very small, and a special arrangement was therefore adopted, requiring that the most restrictive quotas must be raised to three and then to five per cent of home production by the end of the third year from the Treaty's coming into force. Subsequent increases, however, will only be 15%. By the end of the tenth year all quotas must have been increased to not less than 20% of home production.

Any quantitative restrictions on exports as between Member States are to be abolished by the end of the first stage at the latest. These measures are included among provisions to ensure the speediest possible unification of the market in regard to resources as well as sales outlets. Similarly the Treaty provides that state monopolies shall be progressively modified so as to ensure that at the end of the transition period there shall be no discrimination between nationals of the Member States as regards terms of supply and marketing.

THE COMMON EXTERNAL TARIFF

The abolition of customs barriers as between Member States will be accompanied by the progressive establishment of a common tariff towards third countries, so that at the end of the transition period the customs union will have a uniform external tariff. In regard to the level of the external tariff, the General Agreement on Tariffs and Trade (G.A.T.T.) lays it down that the general rate of customs duties in a customs union shall not be higher than the rate which was in force in the countries constituting the union. Hence the external common tariffs must in principle be fixed at the arithmetic mean of the rates of duty applied as between the Member States on 1 January 1957, it being understood that Benelux constituted only one customs area. But the application of this binding rule would in some cases have had consequences conflicting with the economic needs of the Member Countries. So the Treaty, after first clearing up certain technical points in regard to products on which duty had been suspended (*List A*) and in regard to Italian conventional duties,[1] provides that on various groups of products the rate of duty shall be limited to a certain percentage, taking into account the special rules of calculation which tended to raise the average. Moreover, in the case of a number of products enumerated in (*List F*) (*Annex to the Treaty*) the external tariff was fixed at the outset by general agreement in the light of economic needs. Finally there is another list of products (*List G*) which are excluded from the automatic system of calculation and which can be the subject of adjustment and negotiation.

These negotiations must be begun before the end of the second year after the Treaty has come into force, and they must be completed before the end of the first stage.

The procedure for applying the common external

[1]i.e., Customs duties which, by virtue of *conventions* concluded with certain countries, are below the general level of duties.

tariff allows a certain flexibility, provided that it is kept strictly in step with the reduction of the internal tariffs. Where the customs duties were already fairly similar in level, the common tariff will be applied at the end of the fourth year. In the case of other duties, Member States will reduce the difference between their present duties and those laid down in the common tariff by 30% at the end of the first stage and by a further 30% at the end of the second stage. An escape clause allows for the application of the common tariff to be postponed to the extent of five per cent of the value of imports from third countries. In addition, tariff quotas can be authorised by the European Commission[1] under certain very strict conditions, e.g., when the country concerned has been accustomed to obtain supplies from abroad and resources within the Community are inadequate, provided that there is no danger of a shift of activity which would be detrimental to another Member State; these quotas enable the country concerned to import at reduced rates of duty, or free of duty, within the limits fixed by the quota.

Arrangements have been made to prevent any diversion of trade pending the full application of the common customs tariff. Emergency measures can be taken by the Member States.

[1]For an explanation of the 'European Commission', see page 98.

CHAPTER VI

Unification of the Market within the Framework of a Common Policy

AGRICULTURE

SPECIAL arrangements are necessary if agriculture is to be included in an expanded market. The reasons are twofold. In the first place, the abolition of existing protective barriers is liable to have serious repercussions on farm incomes. In the second place, whereas the essential barriers to trade in manufactured products are to be found in customs duties and quantitative restrictions, the same is not true of trade in agricultural products; here, customs duties and quotas are supplemented by all kinds of restrictions, which reflect the varying patterns of agricultural marketing required by the particular social structure of agriculture and its very special conditions of production. There were grounds for wondering whether agricultural products should be included in the Common Market at all if a purely liberal market was out of the question.

But the important role played by agriculture in the economies of several Member States – and particularly in their export trades – led to a decision to include it; it was realised that a balance had to be struck between agriculture's claims for protection and the ultimate advantages which might accrue from an expanded market in the form of stability and higher standards of living in all countries.

Moreover, the exclusion of agriculture would have given rise to a serious maladjustment in the working of the Treaty. It would have been out of the question for industry to be entirely liberalised and subjected to greater competition while agricultural prices could be kept at quite different levels; such a disparity would have had serious effects on wages and production costs. But in view of the involved pattern of the agricultural industry, to which reference has just been made, it was clear that the problem of freeing trade and unifying the market in agriculture, even more than in industry, was not simply a commercial problem but a true problem of integration, with all its social and political ramifications. The result is that for agricultural products (which are listed in Annex II) the Treaty contains special provisions supplementing or amending the general clauses and leading in the direction of an organized market for European agriculture as a whole. And it is against the background of a common agricultural policy that the fusion of the markets is to be accomplished.

The aim of this common policy is:

> To increase agricultural productivity, to ensure a fair standard of living for the agricultural population, to stabilise markets, to guarantee regular supplies and to ensure reasonable prices in supplies to consumers . .

It is not easy to aim at these very different goals at

one and the same time. In fact the Treaty contains three guiding principles on this subject:

> Certain possibilities of protection are to be retained, particularly by means of the minimum price clause, but they are to diminish steadily in the course of time;
>
> Trade within the Community is to be developed, particularly by the conclusion of long-term agreements;
>
> Markets are to be organised, and agricultural production planned on a European scale.

The minimum price clause

In view of the instability of agricultural markets and the fluctuations in agricultural prices it was considered necessary to couple with the freeing of trade a special escape clause which would be both rapid and effective. This is the 'minimum price clause' contained in *Article 44*, the germ of which was already embodied in the Treaty constituting Benelux. If heavy imports should force down agricultural prices on the market of a particular country to a point which might damage its own agriculture, that country would be entitled to fix a minimum price below which all imports would be prohibited. Foreign products would only be admitted if their price was higher.

It would thus be open to each State, by fixing an appropriate minimum price, to frustrate the whole principle of liberation of trade as far as agricultural products were concerned, thereby violating the spirit and aims of the Treaty. This very sweeping provision was therefore supplemented and adjusted by a procedure which required each country to take increasing account of the views of the other countries of the Community and their price levels. A prime task of the organs of the Community will be to work out the bases on which minimum prices are to be calculated; this involves studying the production costs of certain agricultural products within the various countries of the Community and working out what selling price would guarantee a particular income to the farmers concerned whilst giving a reasonable price on the European market. As from the third stage the institutions of the Community will be able to use these agreed base figures as a check on any minimum price applied by a Member State.

Long-term contracts

Besides offering protection against the dislocation of home markets, the Treaty had to stimulate an increase of trade between the members of the Community. Here again, the simple liberal solution of sweeping away tariffs and quotas was considered inadequate, and the drafters of the Treaty had recourse to a stronger stimulus for the development of international trade. Pending the replacement of national organisations by those of the Common Market, the Treaty provides for the signature, before the end of the first stage, of long term agreements which will increase the volume of trade and the prices paid.

If a product is to benefit from long term contracts there must be a surplus in the exporting country and a net deficit in the importing country, and home production in the importing country must be encouraged or protected in some way. This provision really concerns basic products such as wheat, sugar and possibly meat. The prices fixed in the agreements must normally approximate to those paid by the importing country to its own producers on the home market; as the guaranteed prices for home producers are generally higher than those prevailing on export markets this conception of non-discrimination as between the producers of the six countries will give a substantial advantage to the exporting countries.

These long-term contracts are a special arrangement offering some guarantee of an expansion of trade in certain basic products, but their scope will be limited by the need to avoid disturbance to traditional trade channels and by the great differences in price which will still remain. Hence the most interesting aspect of these contracts, from both the economic and political point of view, is their tendency – in the name of the principle of non-discrimination – to establish average European prices which are very close to internal prices.

The common agricultural organisations

But it is the creation of common agricultural organisations or the co-ordination of existing organisations of this kind that will bring unity and development to the European Market. Clearly the organizations must vary considerably according to the products concerned. One may simply enunciate the principle of freedom of trade, laying down a certain number of rules of competition; another, on the contrary, may be an organization having the same structure and the same powers on a European scale as the Wheat Board (O.N.I.C.) has in France for example. Moreover, interests differ from country to country and from product to product. The procedure adopted in creating these common organizations testifies to the prevailing general mood of caution. Negotiations are to be carried out on a basis of unanimity during the first two stages and subsequently by a qualified majority. But the qualified majority has been coupled with a special escape clause entitling countries which find themselves in a minority to ask the Court of Justice for a resumption of the discussion on a basis of unanimity, if it is found that the decision taken by a majority vote affected one of the fundamental aims of the Treaty in the field of agriculture.

Provision was made for a conference of Member States to be called immediately after the Treaty came into force, which would be devoted solely to agriculture; it would draw up a balance sheet to serve as a basis for matching supply and demand on a broad European plane and to give the necessary directives for national efforts. There is no doubt, however, that it will be a delicate and lengthy task to draw up and implement an agricultural policy for the Community. There are innumerable pitfalls in attempting to reconcile the various economic trends and to keep a balance between the various sectors of agriculture. But the aim justifies the effort: the results will be decisive in developing trade and ultimately in bringing price levels in the various countries closer together, with a consequent equalization of production costs and conditions of competition, thus contributing to the fundamental unity of the Common Market and the success of the Treaty as a whole.

TRANSPORT

The decision as to whether transport should be included in the Common Market or not raised the same problems as in the case of agriculture, though to a lesser degree.

It would seem only natural to include transport in the scope of the Treaty of the European Economic Community, with its goals of technical co-operation and fair competition. Moreover, discriminatory transport charges, particularly when goods are reloaded or inspected at the frontier, could easily be a discreet means of wiping out the reduction in customs duties so carefully worked out in other chapters of the Treaty and of seriously distorting the pattern of competition between one country and another.

But whereas economists might be apprehensive of the distorting effects of transport policy, the transport specialists for their part had reasonable grounds to fear that wider economic needs might be invoked to saddle the transport systems with uneconomic charges and unsuitable forms of organisation.

For these reasons the inclusion of transport, as of agriculture, in the Common Market was sought *within the framework of a common policy*, which had first to be worked out. From this principle stem the provisions of the Treaty preparing the way for a common policy under three heads:

> By establishing straight away procedures which would enable decisions to be reached in harmony with the other procedures of the Treaty;
>
> By laying down, within the framework of these procedures, certain broad directives and the objectives which were to be aimed for;
>
> By taking immediate steps to forbid or limit certain practices which offended against the spirit of the Treaty, particularly in regard to fair competition.

In drawing up a common transport policy the Council of Ministers[1] will take certain decisions, which will

[1]For an explanation of the 'Council of Ministers' see page 97.

require unanimity until the end of the second stage, and thereafter will require a qualified majority; these decisions will cover:

a) Common rules governing international transport services originating or terminating in the territory of a Member State or crossing the territory of one or more Member States;

b) The conditions under which non-resident carriers shall be entitled to operate in a Member State;

c) Any other necessary provisions.

However, any provisions which affect the basic transport policies of Member States, and whose application might seriously affect the standard of living and employment in certain regions and the effective use of transport equipment, will be decided upon only by unanimous decision of the Council, bearing in mind the need to adapt transport systems to the economic expansion which will result from the establishment of the Common Market.

Immediate decisions

By the end of the second stage, at the latest, transport undertakings should abolish all discriminatory prices and conditions of carriage based on country of origin or destination of the products concerned. With this end in view the Council, acting by means of a qualified majority, would, within two years from the date on which the Treaty came into force, and after consultation with the Economic and Social Committee, lay down guiding lines within which the Commission would make the necessary decisions after consulting all Member States concerned.

From the start of the second stage, Member States must eliminate from all transport services undertaken within the Community any element of subsidy or protection in prices or conditions of carriage in favour of any particular firms or industries; exceptions will only be permitted if authorised by the Commission. The Treaty does not, however, forbid subsidies which are necessary for the co-ordination of transport or are a compensation for certain drawbacks inherent in the idea of public service.

The foregoing provisions apply only to transport by rail, road and inland waterway; it is merely laid down that the Council of Ministers may, by unanimous decision, raise the questions of air and sea transport, two sectors in which a co-ordination of effort in Europe would be particularly useful. It seems likely that if the Common Market works well in general a powerful impetus will be given to the existing trend towards improved co-operation and harmonization in all sectors of transport.

CHAPTER VII

The Harmonious Working of the Common Market

THE FREE MOVEMENT OF PERSONS, SERVICES AND CAPITAL

To bring about a true fusion and unification of markets, the principles of the Common Market had to be extended progressively to cover such fields as labour and capital in addition to trade. Moreover, if the countries of Europe were to be drawn together, then freedom of movement had to be extended to all classes, and the principle of non-discrimination applied to as many activities as possible. But the free movement of labour and capital and the right of establishment, although indispensable for a true pooling of Europe's resources as a whole and for the long-term operation of mechanisms of economic readjustment, are liable to produce serious social and monetary problems in the short run. It was therefore essential to ensure that these very necessary long-term measures did not cause immediate upheavals.

Labour

The free movement of workers within the Community is to become effective by the end of the transition period at the latest. It implies that each Member State shall abolish all discrimination on grounds of nationality against the workers of other Member States as regards employment, rates of pay and other conditions of work. In particular it implies the right, limited only by the claims of public order and public health, of every worker to accept offers of employment actually made and for this purpose to move or settle freely within the territories of the six Member States.

The Council will determine by simple majority the measures necessary to achieve these aims, including the establishment of machinery for putting workers in contact with employers and for equating labour supply with demand without seriously endangering standards of living and levels of employment in the various regions and industries.

The right of establishment, and paid services

During the transition period restrictions on the right of establishment of nationals of one Member State in the territory of another will be steadily abolished in accordance with a fixed procedure, subject only to limited exceptions. This progressive abolition will also apply to restrictions on the right of subjects of one Member State to set up agencies, branches or subsidiaries on the territory of another. The right of establishment covers the right to enter non-wage-earning occupations and to set up and manage firms and companies.

Before the end of the first stage the Council will lay down, by unanimous decision, a general programme for the abolition of restrictions on the right of establishment. This programme will define for each type of activity the general conditions under which the right of establishment will be introduced and the stages by which this will be done. In implementing this general programme or, in the absence of such a programme, in moving towards the right of establishment in a particular occupation, the Council will take decisions by a unanimous vote up to the end of the first stage and thereafter by a qualified majority. Further, in order to facilitate the introduction of the right of establishment and the exercise of that right, the Council will make arrangements, in accordance with procedures laid down in the Treaty, for the mutual recognition of diplomas, certificates and other qualifications, and for the co-ordination of national legislation on the subject of entry into non-wage-earning occupations and the exercise of such occupations. The same general procedure has been adopted for the abolition of restrictions on payments for services within the Member States of the Community. The word 'services' has a broad meaning, covering insurance, banking and financial activities, distribution and the professions.

Movement of capital

The objectives of the Common Market cannot be fully achieved unless the Community's capital resources can be invested to the best possible advantage. Hence the Treaty provides for the progressive abolition, during the transition period, of restrictions on movements of capital, to the extent which may be necessary for the effective functioning of the Common Market. The Council of Ministers will take the requisite decisions, acting by means of a unanimous vote during the first two stages and by a qualified majority thereafter. An exception is made in the case of loans floated to finance the budget of a Member State or of its public or territorial institutions. The Treaty also contains an escape clause which can be invoked if movements of capital should seriously disturb the working of the capital market of a Member State. This escape clause can, in principle, be invoked only by the Commission, but the Member State concerned may take appropriate preventive or defensive measures on its own initiative, these measures being subsequently examined by the Commission.

The introduction of free movement of capital within the Community inevitably raises certain problems, owing to the different ways in which the Member States treat their relations with third countries. To deal with these problems of exchange control and international movements of capital a procedure for consultation and co-ordination has been laid down; this provides for decisions by a unanimous vote on matters of common legislation, but leaves the way open for any State to take urgent preventive or defensive measures in isolation, subject to the scrutiny of the organs of the Community.

To sum up, these provisions taken as a whole seem to indicate a desire to avoid violent movements of labour or speculative movements of capital in a market which, over the years, has grown accustomed to fragmentation and still displays serious differences in levels of employment and in financial resources. Moreover, as the market grows steadily more unified and conditions in the different countries draw closer together, it will be possible to contemplate the introduction of greater freedom at an earlier stage without running the risk of any serious repercussions. The most interesting feature of the Treaty in this field is perhaps to be found in the phased procedures which leave each State virtually sovereign rights at the start, under the rule of unanimity, but, as the Common Market gets into its stride, gradually give place to increasingly flexible and integrated procedures.

FAIR COMPETITION

There are numerous ways in which competition can be distorted, in which one country can be handicapped in competing with another, or in which the consumer can be deprived of the beneficial effects of competition – in short, there are many ways in which the normal circulation of goods can be impeded. The Treaty comes into action here in three different ways: by its control of agreements and monopolies it ensures that the pooling of markets will be made effective; by controlling the aids or subsidies given in each State it ensures that the market will function fairly; and by correcting distortions which may arise from legislation or regulations imposed on industries it ensures the unity of the market. It is the combination of these controls and the possibilities of harmonization contained in the Treaty which will enable the resulting large market to come into existence without repercussions and to function for the full benefit of all.

Agreements and monopolies

Monopolies exist, and the Treaty does not seek to ban them; it seeks to control their activities so that they will serve the interests of the Community. Hence to take improper advantage of a dominant position is deemed incompatible with the Common Market. Agreements, on the other hand, whether official or secret, present a legal problem. To ban them completely would have the advantage of rendering them null and void, so that any signatory to such an agreement could freely withdraw when he wished. But such a sweeping measure, although it would contain that valuable practical sanction, would fail to take account of the necessities of modern industrial life. Hence substantial loopholes have been left in the Treaty and provision has been made for great flexibility of application.

The Treaty forbids, as running counter to the spirit of the Common Market, all agreements between firms and all concerted practices which are liable to affect trade between Member States and of which the intention or the result is to prevent, restrict or distort competition within the Community; they are therefore declared to be null and void. This clause is aimed in particular at the fixing of prices or other conditions of sale, at practices intended to restrict or control production, sales outlets, the division of markets, etc. But this rule can be waived under certain conditions and in certain cases which help to improve production or distribution or promote technical or economic progress while passing on to the consumer a fair share of the resulting profit.

Within three years from the date on which the Treaty comes into force, the Council, acting by means of a unanimous vote, will lay down any regulations or directives which may be necessary to implement the rules mentioned above. If these measures have not been adopted within the stipulated time they will be enacted by the Council, by means of a qualified majority on the proposal of the Commission and after consultation with the Assembly.

Until the regulations or directives decreed by the Council come into force, national legislation will continue to operate. But the Commission has certain powers of action in this field, from the moment that the Treaty comes into force, including the power to report violations of the principle of fair competition and to authorise any Member State which is harmed by agreements or monopolies in another Member State to take the necessary steps to protect its interests. The Commission is also required to see that public undertakings observe the Treaty. Undertakings which serve the general economic interest or constitute a fiscal monopoly are also subjected in principle to the rules of competition, but with certain restrictions.

Dumping

If at any time during the transition period a Member State or other interested party draws the attention of the Commission to cases of dumping within the Common Market, and if the Commission confirms the allegation, the Commission will make suitable recommendations to the Member State concerned with a view to remedying the position. If the dumping continues, in spite of these recommendations, the Commission may authorise the injured State to take appropriate action for its own protection.

Aids and subsidies

Except where otherwise provided for in the Treaty, governmental aid which may affect trade between Member States is deemed incompatible with the Common Market; this applies to aid of any kind, whether provided by the State or provided from State resources, which may distort competition or threaten to distort it, by giving an advantage to certain undertakings or certain products. The Treaty makes certain immediate exceptions, however, and various types of aid are permitted, such as those intended:

> To stimulate the economies of under-developed regions;
>
> To foster projects which are of benefit to Europe as a whole;
>
> To assist the development of certain activities or certain economic regions without affecting the pattern of trade to the detriment of the public interest.

In regard to the forms of aid already existing when the Treaty comes into force, the Commission will study them with the Member States concerned and will give orders for their abolition if they are deemed incompatible with the principles set out above or if they are improperly applied. Disputes may be referred to the Court of Justice. Member States are required to inform the Commission in advance of any changes which they propose to make to existing forms of aid or any new methods which they propose to introduce.

Harmonization of legislation and correction of distortions

In principle the Treaty does not affect the sovereign rights of Member States in fiscal matters. But certain restrictions on these rights were considered necessary for the effective functioning of the Common Market, and the Treaty therefore contains provisions intended to abolish discrimination, protection and subsidies from the national fiscal systems in regard to relations between Member States. Indirect taxes may be refunded when goods are exported. Under the Treaty the Council, acting by means of a unanimous vote, may require Member States to bring about greater uniformity in any parts of their legislation which have a direct bearing on the establishment or operation of the Common Market.

The Treaty also contains machinery for the elimination of practices which may already distort competition at the time the Treaty comes into force and to prevent new practices of this kind from being created. When, as a result of legislation or government regulations there are differences in the volume of industrial activity, a decision may be made, by a *qualified majority*, to secure greater uniformity in the legislation or regulations concerned, as from the beginning of the second stage. But it was difficult to ensure, for instance, that the social progress made in one State should automatically be extended to all the other States; and it was no less difficult to prevent a State from retaining an adequate degree of autonomy in its own social or fiscal policy. In these circumstances States will be allowed to retain their autonomy, but they will not be entitled to ask for measures to be invoked to correct distortions if they themselves have been responsible for throwing their trade with other countries out of balance by taking independent action against the advice of the European Commission.

CHAPTER VIII

Common Policies

SOCIAL POLICY

THE Common Market already has social implications in that it diminishes differences in social systems and raises standards of living. But the Treaty has more positive social aims, and provision is made for more precise adjustment mechanisms. Differences in working class conditions of life and employment will disappear, as the lower standards are raised; this process will arise partly from the functioning of the Common Market, which will promote a harmonization of social systems, and partly from the procedures laid down in the Treaty and the approximation of laws, regulations and administrative procedures.

The aims of harmonization

The task of the Commission is to promote close collaboration between Member States, particularly in regard to employment, labour legislation, working conditions, vocational training and advancement, social security, protection against occupational accidents and diseases, industrial health, trade union rights and collective bargaining between employers and workers. To this end the Commission works in close contact with Member States, carrying out research, giving opinions and arranging consultations, in regard to national and international problems. Before giving its opinions the Commission will consult the Economic and Social Committee.

In certain regards it did not seem enough to rely on the general effects of the Treaty or on the formulation of long-term objectives, and provision was made for timetables or clear-cut procedures for harmonizing social policy. Under the Treaty each Government pledges itself to apply during the first stage of the transition period the principle of equal pay for men and women and to maintain the existing relationships between the systems of paid holidays. In addition, in the special protocol concerning France, Member States record their opinion that at the end of the first stage after the establishment of the Common Market a situation will have been reached in which the basic level for overtime payment and the average overtime rates of pay will correspond to those which existed in France, according to the average figures for 1956. If at the end of that period these conditions have not been realised, the institutions of the Community must provide a suitable escape clause for French industries suffering as a result of this inequality.

The European Social Fund

It was realised that the freedom of movement offered to workers might prove to be illusory if the workers lacked the resources to enable them to seek the best possible employment, and that it might also cause serious local disturbances. Hence a European Social Fund was set up to facilitate the transfer of workers to other employment, as part of the policy of adapting national economies to the large market. On the request of a Member State the Fund will meet 50% of any payments which are made by that State, or by a public body, from the time the Treaty comes into force, in order to provide for workers:

A vocational retraining to fit unemployed workers for productive employment of a different nature, if no other work can be found for them and provided that they are subsequently employed for not less than six months in the occupation for which they have been retrained.

Resettlement expenses to enable unemployed workers to take up productive employment of a different nature, if they have been forced to change their residence within the Common Market and if they have subsequently been engaged in productive employment in their new place of residence for not less than six months.

Grants to enable them to maintain the same wage-level pending their full re-employment after their previous employment has been temporarily reduced or suspended, wholly or partly as a result of the change-over of the employing firm to other production; this measure is subject to the conditions that the workers must subsequently have been fully employed again for a period of at least six months, and that the government concerned must have submitted a reconversion plan which must have been approved by the European Commission.

The European Social Fund has a limited scope, partly because its financial contribution only covers 50%

of the outlay made by the Member States, and partly because it can only contribute to the expenses of workers who have already found new employment; there is thus no question of the Fund accepting full liability for employment problems within the Community; it is merely a mechanism intended to facilitate the necessary adjustments.

It is possible that the common social policy will produce its most interesting developments when the authorities responsible for social questions are brought together through the medium of the Common Market and involved in a permanent exchange of views, particularly within the institutions of the Community. The signature of the Social Security Convention for workers migrating within the six countries foreshadows these developments.

THE COMMON ECONOMIC POLICY

In economic as in social matters the guiding principle of the Treaty is to rely on the virtues inherent in the large market and on the wisdom of the common institutions which will supervise its application, but at the same time to establish at the outset certain compensatory mechanisms to assist that application and to guide it towards a fair sharing of opportunities as between the regions.

Corrections and safeguards

The harmonization processes are intended to pave the way to a common economic policy by stimulating agreement on the most sensitive points. Other provisions in the Treaty, although they may have negative or safeguarding aspects, are intended to encourage a collective economic outlook and thus to correct the relatively automatic working of the mechanisms which create the customs union. The timing of the various operations reflects the gradualism of the Treaty and the possibilities of flexibility in its application, which are essential counterparts to its irrevocability. Geographically, *Article 226* enables appropriate safeguarding action to be taken if the working of the Common Market should throw the economy of any areas seriously out of balance. This provision reflects particularly clearly the aim of the Treaty set out in *Article 2*: 'the harmonious development of economic activities throughout the Community'. Finally, the rules governing competition reflect an anxiety to avoid damage to the market of one Member State as a result of unfair practices by firms located in another Member State.

The positive role of the common external tariff

Once the initial disparities have been corrected, and it is no longer necessary to resort to the safeguarding measures mentioned above, the rational development of economic activity within the Community will be based on the existence of a common external tariff towards third countries, supplemented by a common trade policy; on the institution of procedures of consultation and co-ordination at the highest level; and on the adoption of joint machinery to deal with external payments and internal investments.

A common customs tariff is a powerful factor in equalising competitive conditions and production costs in the industries of the six countries. The prices of imported raw materials, semi-finished goods and manufactures will be equalised. Within this framework of uniform protection there will be less to fear from serious disparities in economic development. The joint commercial policy, which has to pay due regard to the interests of each of the member countries, will tend to increase the cohesion of their economies and to encourage them to seek a balance in domestic production and standards of living. During the transition period the Member States must take steps to co-ordinate their trading relations with third countries so that by the end of that period the foundations will have been laid upon which a common policy in foreign trade can be built. A procedure for negotiation and decision has been carefully worked out which involves acting by a qualified majority as from the third stage and shares the responsibilities between the Council of Ministers and the European Commission.

Internal and external monetary problems

Although the Treaty binds the Member States closely together in matters of trade, it leaves them complete autonomy in the monetary sphere; each State keeps its own currency and continues to be responsible for maintaining its own balance of payments. It should be noted that the requirements of monetary policy closely determine a State's attitude towards its foreign trade; hence, if the Common Market is to function effectively, a certain co-ordination of monetary policies is essential. The Treaty lays down two very general objectives: stability and balance. But to achieve these objectives may be a matter of some delicacy. The Treaty merely requires Member States to co-ordinate their economic policies and ensure that there is collaboration between their appropriate administrative services and between their central banks. In addition, it establishes a Monetary Committee, of an advisory character, which will be responsible for watching the monetary and financial situation of the Member States and reporting regularly to the institutions of the Community. It is also laid down that 'each Member State shall treat its policy in regard to rates of exchange as a problem of common interest'.

Those who drafted the Treaty could not overlook the possibility that a State might be confronted with serious difficulties in its balance of payments owing to the establishment of the Common Market or for some other reason. If it were threatened by a persistent deficit that State would have only two possibilities open to it: either to defend itself once again by restricting its imports or to obtain help from its partners while applying the necessary internal measures to restore the situation. The second of these solutions is the one which the Treaty tends to favour. A procedure is laid down for 'confirming the existence' of the situation, after which the institutions of the Community may grant mutual aid to the State which is in difficulties, even going so far as to call on the other Member States for loans. If those States were to refuse to give mutual aid, the institutions of the Community would be required to provide an escape clause for the State which was in difficulties. Notwithstanding the general provisions, however, in the case of a sudden balance of payments crisis the Member State concerned may of its own initiative take the necessary measures of safeguard to meet the situation, subject to verification by the institutions of the Community.

These various solutions bear the stamp of caution. Their 'transitional' character is sometimes evident. At the time of the signature of the Treaty the machinery of the European Payments Union had already established a certain balance in credits and settlements, whilst there was some doubt as to the need for monetary co-ordination in view of the development of the Common Market. Since then the abolition of the European Payments Union on 1st January, 1959, and the moves toward convertibility made by the major European countries have strengthened the position of the individual European currencies and of Europe as a whole in regard to external payments. Nevertheless, unless there is a return to general and complete convertibility, an extension of solidarity among the six countries in this sphere will still be valuable and may prove to be indispensable.

Internal economic equilibrium

In the field of internal economic policy it was felt necessary to arrange in advance not only the procedures to be followed but also the more detailed machinery to control the possible effects of the expansion of the market. The Treaty sets up a European Investment Bank with a capital of 1,000 million dollars and with a legal personality quite separate from that of the Community, in which the States signatory to the Treaty will be the shareholders. The function of the European Investment Bank is to contribute to the smooth and balanced development of the Common Market in the interests of the Community, calling on the capital markets and on its own resources. It will make loans and guarantees, on a non-profit-making basis, to facilitate the financing of the following types of projects in all sectors of the economy:

Projects for developing the less advanced regions;

Projects for modernising or converting enterprises or creating new activities, where such action is beyond the financial resources of one State;

Projects which are of common concern to several Member States but which, owing to their size or their nature, cannot be entirely financed from the resources of the States concerned.

The function of the Bank is thus to focus the common investment policy linked to the development of the Common Market; it provides the means for carrying out this policy, but its function should not be misunderstood. The Bank does not aim to take over responsibility for all investment in the six countries. Its role is one of guidance and encouragement. The extent of its resources and the procedure for reaching decisions which is laid down in its constitution will allow it to correct or compensate, where necessary, the existing operation of investment mechanisms and the excessive concentrations to which they might give rise, but not to take their place.

The role of the institutions

Lastly, provision is made for permanent consultation and co-ordination within the institutions of the Community; these provisions range from general principles (co-ordination of economic policies, financial implications of decisions made by organs of the Community, trends of economic policy) to more clearly defined tasks and procedures under each of the specialised chapters of the Treaty (movements of capital, balance of payments, rates of exchange, agriculture, transport). As has already been pointed out, explicit provision has been made in these two fields, the general and the specialised, for the functioning and development of the

Common Market to be linked to the establishment of a common policy. In regard to the movement of labour and the freedom of establishment, the necessary balances can be ensured by compensating mechanisms or by the existence of an agreed overall plan. Finally, the Council of Ministers, in conjunction with the other organs of the institutions – Assembly, Economic and Social Committee and European Commission – will provide a forum for a permanent interchange of national viewpoints and will permit the formulation of the broad outlines of a concerted plan of action both within the Community and in the sphere of foreign relations.

There is no gainsaying the fact that these procedures leave certain gaps in the pattern of economic unification, and they do not entirely guarantee internal and external equilibrium; but at the present stage it was not easy to envisage fuller or more binding measures. Investment policies and autonomy in monetary matters, in particular, are two such essential ingredients in political independence and in power relationships that the unity and solidarity of the six countries could not be immediately increased without seriously prejudicing the essentially political developments of the Common Market.

If the working of the Common Market should reveal a need for more or stronger measures, in the monetary sphere, for instance, they can be discussed in the institutions and, if necessary, decided. The Council of Ministers, acting by means of a unanimous vote, on the proposal of the Commission and after consulting the Assembly, can take appropriate action. *Article 235* expressly lays this down as the procedure to be followed if some further common action should prove necessary in order to achieve one of the goals of the Community, even though the form which such action should take has not been defined and written in to the Treaty.

CHAPTER IX

The Institutions of the Community and Association with Overseas Territories

A. THE INSTITUTIONS OF THE COMMUNITY

THE system of institutions laid down in the Treaty of Rome is distinguished from that of the Coal and Steel Community by its less supra-national character. Whereas in the E.C.S.C. the real power is vested in the High Authority, a purely 'European' body, in the European Economic Community the power of decision is entrusted, in the majority of cases, to a Council made up of ministers representing the governments of the Member States.

It was felt necessary, however, to ensure the existence and authority of a supra-national institution, independent of the national States, which would be both the protector of the Treaty and the moving spirit behind it. This of course reflected the wishes of the more convinced 'Europeans', but it also reflected the anxieties of the lesser powers. Thus, the Commission (the equivalent of the High Authority in the E.C.S.C.) has certain prerogatives which counterbalance those of the Council and which have the effect of ensuring a permanent co-operation between the two organs, one of which considers problems from the Community point of view while the other lays more stress on the national concerns of the Member States. The Council and the Commission are assisted by various consultative committees, and their actions are supervised by an Assembly. Finally, there is a Court of Justice which ensures that the terms of the Treaty are justly carried out.

The Council of Ministers

The Council is composed of a representative of the government of each State. Its task is to co-ordinate the economic policy of the Member States with that of the Community. In the majority of cases – and the most important ones – the Council acts on the proposal of the Commission. This is an innovation, intended to ensure that at the vital points in the working of the Community the proposals upon which the representatives of the Member States are required to decide shall always be initiated by the Commission, the watchdog of the Community. On the other hand there are circumstances in which the Council, a political organ, will have the right to quash the decisions of the Commission, to which it forms a sort of court of ratification or appeal.

It is mainly in the first two stages of the Common Market that the Council reaches its decisions by majority vote, and in those cases which are of a predominantly political character. But the qualified majority is the normal procedure under the Treaty, particularly in cases where approval is to be given to a proposal made by the Commission. Under this system seventeen votes are divided among the six Member States as follows: France, Germany and Italy, four votes each, Belgium and

Holland two votes each, Luxembourg one vote; the majority is fixed at twelve votes, or just over two thirds. The effect of this weighting is to prevent any two great powers from outvoting a third great power without the support of both Belgium and Holland.

The European Commission consists of nine members and may not include more than two members of the same nationality. The members of the Commission are not representatives of States. They are independent, they may not take instructions from any source, and they act only 'in the interests of the Community'. They are appointed on the unanimous agreement of the governments for a period of four years and they may be re-elected. They are subject to the doctrine of collective responsibility and their decisions are made by simple majority. The powers of the Commission can be grouped in four categories. In the first place it is the body responsible for ensuring that Member States carry out the provisions of the Treaty: for this purpose it is empowered to make recommendations and give opinions. In the second place the Commission is the body which represents the Community – before the Assembly (to which it is responsible), in judicial matters, and in negotiations with third countries and with international organisations. It has powers of independent decision, being able to carry out measures within the general framework laid down by the Treaty or to take action on behalf of the Community in cases of urgency (escape clauses). Finally, the Commission shares the Council's powers of decision by virtue of its 'right of proposal' which is exercised under the conditions indicated above.

The members of *The Economic and Social Committee* are drawn from the branches of economic and social life affected by the working of the Common Market; they are nominated by Member States and appointed by the Council. The Committee is required to contain two specialised groups for transport and agriculture respectively, the two fields in which the development of the Common Market depends particularly upon subsequent decisions of the institutions of the Community. The Treaty defines the circumstances in which the Committee must be consulted. Provision is also made for consultation with other specialised committees of a more technical nature.

The Assembly is the body which exercises political control over the institutions of the Community. It is made up of delegates chosen by the parliaments of the Member States from amongst their numbers, and in accordance with their own procedure, which may vary from country to country. The Assembly is entitled to put to the Commission written and oral questions to which the Commission, as the organ representing the Community, must reply; and the Commission must submit an annual report to the Assembly. The Assembly has the right to force the resignation of the Commission by means of a vote of censure.

The Court of Justice is composed of seven judges appointed by the unanimous agreement of the Member States. Its task is to ensure that the Treaty is validly applied and interpreted, and by virtue of this mandate it adjudicates in disputes between Member States, between Member States and the organs of the Community, or in appeals against the organs of the Community.

A convention annexed to the Treaty lays it down that the Assembly and the Court of Justice shall be common to the three Communities of which the six countries are members: the Coal and Steel Community, the Atomic Energy Community (Euratom) and the Common Market.

TRANSITION FROM ONE STAGE TO THE NEXT

The institutions are intended to keep a permanent check on the smooth running of the Treaty, and they have been given considerable discretionary powers. There is only one item for which a special procedure has been laid down in advance: the transition from the first to the second stage. This is the point at which the effects of the Treaty will begin to make themselves clearly felt and the whole future of the Common Market will be in the balance. Moreover, in a number of cases the second stage marks the introduction of certain majority decisions. The transition from the first to the second stage will be dependent upon a confirmatory statement to the effect that the essential objectives laid down for the first stage have been effectively attained. This statement will be made at the end of the fourth year by the Council, acting by means of a unanimous vote. If unanimity cannot be achieved the first stage may be extended for two years, or three years at the most. But there is a possibility of appeal to an arbitration tribunal. The second and third stages can be prolonged or shortened by the Council acting by means of a unanimous vote, but the passage from one stage to another, and from the transition to the permanent period, is automatic.

ESCAPE CLAUSES

Unbalanced application of the Treaty is precluded *a priori* by the fact that it is to be brought into operation gradually over a long period, and by the machinery provided for the transition from one stage to the next. Nevertheless, recourse to escape clauses may be necessary during the application of the Treaty. These clauses cover such matters as the balance of payments position of a Member-State, dumping and the manipulation of trade channels, – *i.e.*, the possibility that a country outside the Community may make use of a Member State in order to flood the market of another Member State; this is a possibility which will exist until the common external tariff has been fully implemented and as long as there are any important differences in trade policy between the Member States, particularly in regard to quotas. As a rule the scope and nature of the steps to be taken under these escape clauses are not clearly defined; in most cases the Commission is left to make suitable proposals. In cases of urgency Member States can take the necessary steps unilaterally, leaving the institutions of the Community to approve or disapprove by a qualified majority. There are also more specific escape clauses which provide a means of waiving certain rules or objectives for liberalization in regard to particular chapters (movement of capital, labour, etc.). Finally, the Treaty also contains a general escape clause which can be invoked during the transition period in the case of serious difficulties which may be liable to persist in any particular sector of the economy or to endanger the economic stability of any region. Only the Commission can give authority for this clause to be invoked.

B. ASSOCIATION WITH OVERSEAS TERRITORIES

The political and economic links existing between certain Member States and certain large territories outside Europe, particularly in Africa, could be regarded either as an obstacle to the creation of a customs union in Europe or as an opportunity for Europe to create a closer Community between Europe and Africa. It was the second view which prevailed. But another problem arose from the fact that these extra-European countries are mostly under-developed and may place a considerable financial burden on the metropolitan countries. It finally appeared that the most effective form of association was to be found in a joint investment policy, to supplement the efforts already made by certain States, coupled with a development of reciprocal trade between the States of the Community and the overseas countries and territories. The general principles of this association were written in to the Treaty. A Convention which is annexed to the Treaty sets out the steps to be taken *during an initial period* of five years. Before the expiry of this Convention the Council, acting by means of a unanimous vote, will draw up the provisions for a further period in the light of the experience already gained.

The Common Investment Fund

The Convention provides for the setting up of a Development Fund for the Overseas Countries and Territories, to which all Member States will contribute. Through this Fund the Community will help to provide finance for welfare projects and for public works which are directly linked with definite productive development projects. The 'vetting' of projects and the allocation of funds are carried out under a Community procedure, and the funds are placed at the disposal of the authorities responsible for carrying out the projects. Over a period of five years the European States will contribute a total of 580 million dollars to this Fund, on an annually increasing scale.

Customs duties and quotas

An increased liberalisation of trade will go hand in hand with the provision of financial aid. Increased trade between the States of the Community and the overseas countries and territories involves the abolition of customs duties and quotas on goods passing in both directions. The Convention indicates how the general principles of the Treaty are to be applied to the progressive removal of customs duties and abolition of quantitative restrictions. But the States of the Community have recognised that the special economic needs of the overseas countries and territories may required the maintenance or imposition of a customs tariff, either to protect growing industry or to ensure the necessary tax revenue for budgetary purposes. If it should prove necessary to retain or modify tariffs on these lines, the prescribed reduction of duties will be carried out in such a way as to bring them down to the level of the duties imposed on products imported from the Member State which has special relations with the overseas country or territory concerned; the object is to ensure that by the end of the transition period the States of the Community will be on an equal footing. In regard to quantitative restrictions the broad lines of the Treaty will be applied in the relations between Member States and overseas countries and territories, subject to certain differences in methods of calculation. It should also be noted that provision is made for nationals of the Member States to establish themselves in the overseas countries and territories.

As we have already mentioned, at the end of the five year period the Council of Ministers will decide (by a unanimous vote) what action is to be taken in regard to the system established by the first Convention. Until these measures are decided upon, there will be no change in import quotas or in the rules governing the right of establishment of nationals and companies of Member States. Tariff reductions will continue according to plan, as will the building up of the common external tariff on all products. The level of the common external tariff on the principal overseas products has been fixed so as to give local producers the benefit of a wide market in Europe without interfering with traditional channels of trade (tariff quotas at reduced rates of duty have already been established in certain cases: bananas, coffee . . .); the object here is to facilitate economic development and raise standards of living in the producing countries themselves.

PART III

The Common Market and its Application

CHAPTER X

The Basic Factors

THE six countries forming the Common Market have many affinities. This means, in the first place, that they have common frontiers, but it also implies that they are completely comparable in structure. Their economic and social development since the nineteenth century has followed broadly the same lines although the pace may have varied. Their way of life is similar, and by world standards, or even by the standards of Europe as a whole, the differences in their standards of living are very small. The degree of integration – the extent to which agricultural and industrial products are inter-changed amongst the six countries – is already considerable, and there are also many links between individual firms. They share the same political principles. These general indications are in line with the idea of an *optimum* area of application which has already been mentioned in regard to the possibility of achieving a common market. They appear even more impressive when the resources of the six constituent countries are added together. These factors must not, however, be allowed to mask the divergences which also exist.

THE BALANCE-SHEET OF RESOURCES

In 1958 the population of the Common Market countries was 167 million (Federal Republic of Germany 52·5; Italy 48·9; France 44·8; Holland 11·3; Belgium 9·1; Luxembourg 0·3), placing the European Economic Community in the same rank as the two greatest world powers: U.S.S.R. 209 million, U.S.A. 178 million.

As far as *working* population is concerned (1958) the Community outnumbers the United States: U.S.S.R. 89 million; E.E.C. 74 million; U.S.A. 69 million.

In the sphere of agricultural production (wheat, milk, meat, etc.) the Common Market occupies a leading position in several sectors and the high production figures are matched by a particularly high consumption. On the other hand, the Community is almost entirely dependent on foreign sources for supplies of agricultural products for industrial use, such as rubber and cotton. It is only in the case of certain imported foodstuffs such as rice, cocoa, and coffee, that the Overseas Territories can make any really appreciable contribution.

In industrial production the aggregated figures for the six countries make an impressive showing. They represent more than 20% of the world's production of bauxite, potash and phosphates, and between 10% and 20% of its iron, lead and nickel production. If comparison is limited to the figures for steel production alone (which are a good index of industrial capacity), the strength of the six countries is seen to be comparable with that of the U.S.A. or the U.S.S.R.:

Steel Production (1958)

U.S.A.	77 million tons
E.E.C.	58 million tons
U.S.S.R.	55 million tons

This comparative picture is completed by a comparison of the gross power consumption (given as tons of coal, 1956):

U.S.A.	1,356 million tons
E.E.C.	416 million tons
U.S.S.R.	415 million tons

The total production in the six Common Market countries of aluminium, cement, textiles and motor vehicles can again be compared with that of the two great powers: the E.E.C. equals and even surpasses the U.S.S.R. in several fields such as the production of electricity, textiles and vehicles.

Production of vehicles (1958) (in thousands)

U.S.A.	4,247
E.E.C.	2,600
U.S.S.R.	212

On the other hand, the figures relating to *income* and *gross national product* are appreciably lower than those for the U.S.A. In 1957 the total gross national product for the six countries (156 thousand million dollars) was only some 40% of that of the U.S.A.

In *world* trade the union of the six countries occupies a more important position than the U.S.A. and runs level with the entire sterling area:

Figures for 1959 in thousand million dollars

	Imports	*Exports*
World trade	104·4	99·9
U.S.A.	15·0	17·4
E.E.C.	24·1	25·2
Sterling area, including Great Britain	24·8	21·5 (1958)
Great Britain	11·2	9·3

As importers of foodstuffs and raw materials the Community accounts for some 31% of world trade, the United States 16%, the United Kingdom 18%. In other words, the market which the Community offers for these products is almost double that of the United States and two-thirds larger than that of the United Kingdom.

As an exporter of industrial products it accounts for about 33% of world trade as against the 26% of the United States and the 16% of the United Kingdom. In other words, its sales are double those of the United Kingdom and almost 30% greater than those of the United States.

Turning to origin and destination, we note that a large part of the Community's trade in primary products consists of exchanges within the Community and of imports coming from the United States, whereas the United States offers no market for primary products from the Community. The sales of manufactured products within the Community are almost four times as great as those achieved by the member-countries in the United States.

Lastly, if trade between the countries of the Community, the United States and the United Kingdom is excluded, in order to gauge the significance of these three great trading partners for the rest of the world, it will be seen that exports of manufactures from America to the rest of the world still exceed those of the Community, which in turn exceed British exports by 40%; but as a buyer of primary products from these areas, the Community already has a lead of one-third over the United States, whose purchases are barely larger than those of the United Kingdom.

The six countries trade very extensively with each other so that the pattern of trade is already relatively integrated.

The Common Market's Share in 1958

	of imports into	*of exports from*
Belgium and Luxembourg	47%	46%
Netherlands	44%	44%
Germany	29%	27%
Italy	26%	27%
France	26%	27%

On a percentage basis it appears that the Netherlands and the Union of Belgium and Luxembourg are most dependent on the other countries of the Community; but these are perhaps the countries for which trade with third countries is most essential; and the fact that France appears to be less integrated with the Community than the other countries can be directly ascribed to the importance of its trade with the Overseas Territories. Hence, the above statistics give an imperfect picture of the fundamental pattern of trade of the six countries. Similarly, global statistics, although they produce impressive figures of production or trade, ignore these underlying divergences in the structure of the member-States.

THE FACTORS MAKING FOR DIVERGENCE

The following table shows the gross national product per inhabitant for each country in the Community, for the year 1957:

	In dollars
Germany	1,120
Belgium	1,170
France	1,080
Italy	600
Netherlands	980

The gross national product is made up as follows:

	Agri-culture	*Industry including building*	*Services*
Germany (Federal Republic) ..	9	51	40
Belgium	7	47	46
France	15	41	44
Italy	22	42	36
Luxembourg	9	54	37
Netherlands	11	44	45

France alone accounts for more than one-third of the *agricultural* production of the six. Italy and Germany each account for one-quarter, Netherlands 8%, Belgium 6%. These differences in the part played by agriculture in the economy of each country can be set alongside considerable differences in productivity, as is shown by the statistics for two typical products given below:

	Germany	*France*	*Italy*	*Belgium Luxembourg*	*Netherlands*
Wheat yield (cwts. per acre 1952–55)	21·5	17·5	14	26	30·5
Annual yield of milk per cow in gallons (1952–55) ..	638	462	383	812	853

Thus, the countries with the largest agricultural production are often the least productive in regard to yield (and the least specialised). In working out a balance between production and exchange, however, we must give them considerable weight, whilst bearing in mind the requirements of specialisation. Moreover, there are variations in price-levels; prices in France are higher for certain products such as milk and butter (particularly by comparison with prices in Holland), whilst the home price of wheat in France is lower than in Germany where production is heavily protected and subsidised. Finally, the methods of protection and, more generally, of State intervention in agricultural markets, are as varied as they are difficult to modify.

With regard to *industry*, the production of the six countries in 1957 can be estimated at 70·6 thousand million dollars, made up as follows:

Germany	41%
France	28%
Italy	17%
Belgium-Luxembourg	7%
Netherlands	7%

But Germany's considerable industrial power is not reflected in the standard of living or *per capita* consumption of her population, Belgium and France being in the lead in these respects. This is due to various factors: a more rapid recovery after the war in certain countries (sometimes followed by a certain stagnation, as in Belgium), lower prices in others (Netherlands), lack of progress in certain areas (Mezzagiorno) in Italy.

The reasons for the variations in prices are extremely complicated: divergences in wages or social charges, the incidence of taxation, the burden of distribution costs – all these provide a partial explanation. Taking wages and social charges as a whole, Germany does not appear to be in a particularly advantageous position apart from certain exceptional sectors; and the same applies to the global tax figures.

Taxation compared for the year 1956

As a percentage:	*Germany*	*France*	*Italy*	*Belgium*	*Netherlands*	*Luxembourg*
of the gross national income at wholesale prices	40	41	42	29	37	38
of the gross national income at market prices ..	32	31	30	24	30	29
of the gross national product, at market prices plus internal transfers ..	29	27	25	21	28	26

The first conclusion revealed by these figures is that taxation as a whole is high in all the countries of the Community, although appreciably less so in Belgium. The difference in the relative incidence of taxation, depending on whether it is calculated on wholesale or market prices, clearly shows the predominance of indirect taxes and charges in France and Italy, which have the effect of increasing the apparent taxation figure as a proportion of net income. The difference in the relative incidence of taxation according to whether the gross national product is taken alone or increased by the addition of internal transfers, again demonstrates the importance of transfers financed by taxation in France and Italy.

Thus, from the industrial point of view, and more generally from the point of view of economic activity, there appear to be no very serious divergences in the potential competitive power of the various countries, (apart from straightforward comparisons of volume and except in the case of southern Italy); but many differences appear in the relationships between one sector and another and in the numerous elements which, taken as a whole, give a more or less adequate balance. Even if we take into consideration prices, wages, social charges, taxation systems, the progress made by particular branches of industry or the improvements effected in their productivity, in every case the part these factors play is varied, as – more often than not – are the techniques employed. This is not an obstacle to the initial application of the Common Market but it will raise certain increasingly delicate problems of harmonisation as the application proceeds.

All the factors considered above are merely different aspects of a monetary, economic and social policy, whose scope ranges from the control of savings to the structure of channels of distribution, and which has hitherto been strictly national. There is, of course, an external parallel in the balance of payments, for example, which starts from an extremely unfavourable position in France and from a favourable – perhaps even too favourable – position in Germany. But it is unnecessary to go into the details of the mechanism by which price levels, currency and the balance of payments position tend to react on each other; the case of France has shown that the payments position was primarily a consequence, assuming various forms, rather than a permanent cause of difficulties, and that the real foundations of ultimate success in large-scale competition must be laid at home.

THE CASE OF FRANCE

At the time when the Treaty of Rome was signed, France was in an economic situation which exposed her to considerable criticism, and even more considerable doubt as to her competitive potentialities. French prices (and those in the franc zone generally) were often estimated to be almost 20% higher than in other countries. In 1956 the deficit in the French balance of payments had reached 830 million dollars, largely on trading account, and of this some 25% was attributable to the Overseas Territories. The balance of trade was characterised by a very heavy deficit in fuel and power, an increasing dependence on foreign sources for raw materials, semi-manufactured products and capital goods, and a relatively low export of finished products (29% of French exports as against 42% of German exports). Although trade with the five countries of the Common Market is steadily increasing (and reducing, in particular, the dominant position held by trade with the Overseas Territories) it still makes a poor showing in regard to the more finished types of agricultural and industrial products.

Turning to the existing level of protection, it should be noted that, in addition to a fairly high customs tariff, France had in practice been obliged to place almost the whole of her foreign trade under a quota system. Hence, in order to keep her foreign trade in balance and prevent the loss of foreign exchange, she had had to waive the rules of the O.E.E.C. itself. This situation explains the caution displayed by the French negotiators and also the fears expressed by public opinion at the prospect of further considerable commitments to reduce customs and quota barriers.

It was easy to think that in the fairly near future the operation of the Treaty of Rome would be particularly disadvantageous to France, seen solely from the point of view of the balance of foreign trade. Since the participants in the Common Market had all liberalised their trade to a much greater extent (over 90% by the O.E.E.C. standard) and their level of customs duties was often lower, it was in France that the clauses for the lowering of trade barriers would have the most immediate and tangible effect. In particular, the clause which provided for the automatic fixing of quotas equal to 3% of national production in cases where these did not exist or were very low, affected several highly protected but very important sectors (motor vehicles, cotton cloth, radio or television sets). The operation of the Treaty could by itself lead in a few years to a four or five-fold increase in the imports of these products, and to an additional deficit of the order of 130 to 140 thousand million.

On the other hand, it was difficult to see the factors which would restore the balance. Agricultural exports can only be increased slowly and the operation of the Treaty could only produce such an increase very gradually and partially. Moreover, the application of the general clauses for harmonisation in the social or economic fields was liable to be postponed or was not clearly defined; this applied equally to the institution of a common tariff, to wages and to the burden imposed by Overseas Territories.

Such judgments were based on a purely static, and therefore erroneous, view of economic processes. Moreover, there is no doubt that the Common Market has provided the opportunity for a complete change in the economic policy of France, an indirect, but not inconsiderable effect of the Treaty.

It is always difficult to assess psychological factors, and even more difficult to foresee them. Nevertheless, it could reasonably be assumed that the development of trade would not all be on one side and that increased purchases abroad would have a contagious effect on sales. The private sector of the French economy, confronted by the inescapable requirements of the Common Market and aware of the fact that the Treaty did after all include certain guarantees to offset the risks, appears to have responded in a most positive fashion.

This favourable response by individual firms was made possible and accentuated by a transformation which took place in France's general position. Some days before the first steps were taken in the application of the Treaty, on the 27th December, 1958, France carried out a monetary and economic reform of the greatest importance. At the same time, a successful devaluation resulted in more realistic rates of exchange and facilitated exports; trade was liberalised, up to a proportion of 90% in the first instance, a level comparable with that achieved by the other participants in the Common Market. Thus, in a climate of monetary stability, reinforced by the effect of the liberalisation of trade on internal prices, the normal conditions of international competition were restored.

It then became evident that the internal situation in France, seen from the economic point of view, could well bear comparison with that of her neighbours – a situation which had previously been obscured by payments difficulties.

For ten years France had been carrying out a policy of capital investment, increasing productive capacity and making it possible for her to increase exports without setting up inflationary pressures. The announcement of the Common Market, and the fact that people believed in it, were instrumental in calling forth the necessary efforts towards regrouping and additional specialisation, and transforming psychological attitudes.

CHAPTER XI

The Prospects for Equilibrium

THE capacities of the various countries and the attitudes of their individual citizens have not, of course, lost any of their importance. But it is not sufficient merely to tidy up a situation; the possibilities it offers must be sustained and developed. The opportunities which the Treaty offers for a long-term equilibrium thus depend on two considerations:

- the general pattern of economic activity in each country, taking into account the most permanent factors involved;
- the operation of the Treaty as it affects the harmonisation of the national policies of each of the six countries.

For example, there is at the present time a deficit – taking the Community as a whole – in various sectors of agriculture. All the countries, with the exception of France, are net importers of cereals. France and the Netherlands are the only net exporters of meat, eggs and butter. If a balance sheet is drawn up for the total food resources of the Common Market it will be found that only the Netherlands have an export surplus, France and

Italy are virtually self-supporting, whilst Germany and the Union of Belgium and Luxembourg have deficits of the order of 25%.

Nevertheless, France and the franc zone still play a very small part in meeting these requirements (less than 20%).

French exports of butter cover only 8% of the requirements of the importing countries, exports of cheese less than 2% and of vegetables 12%; in the case of fruit France is even a net importer. With regard to the Overseas Territories, although they supply more than 40% of the five countries' requirements in cocoa, the figure ranges from nil to about 1% in the case of coffee, bananas and ground-nuts.

The figures for manufactures are even lower, 15% in the case of chemicals and 11% in the case of capital goods. The French contribution towards meeting the needs of the Common Market is still too much in the form of raw materials.

France has been taken here as an example. Each of the member-countries can undertake the same analysis and make the appropriate deductions regarding the advantages to be gained from changes in the pattern of its economic activities. Assuming that the present rate of increase in consumption continues over the next ten years, *per capita* consumption in 1971 would be 50% higher than in 1955, even under the system of compartmentalised national economies. If we allow for the increase in population and the progress which may be expected to follow from the fusion of the six economies, it is not unreasonable to suggest that today's total consumption figures may have *doubled* by 1970.

But this increase in consumption will vary from sector

to sector. Recent statistical surveys suggest that, whereas the average increase will be 100%, the increase in the various sectors will be as follows: foodstuffs 50%; clothing 100%; housing 60%; durable consumer goods 200%; miscellaneous and services 150%. This is only a very rough estimate, but it serves to show that in the long run the increase in the demand for manufactured products will be greater than that for agricultural products, owing to the relatively inelastic nature of the demand for foodstuffs.

Again, taking France as an example, there are other important factors which must be taken into account in determining the conditions necessary for maintaining a state of equilibrium within the Community: first the increase in the working population of France during future years; secondly the possibility of reducing France's basic deficit in hydrocarbons and power supplies. But the position of any national economy in the economy of the Common Market will depend above all on a continued effort of investment and modernisation.

But although an increase in French imports can already be forecast, this increase will keep within the limits of internal demand and of French financial resources, both of which are directly related to the national income, i.e., the increase in French internal production. Moreover, the extent to which French demand will be met by French products and the products of the other member countries respectively depends not only on price levels and the degree of specialisation achieved but also on the rate of exchange which, as the Treaty stands at present, is fixed by each State at its sole discretion. But rates of exchange cannot be fixed without regard to the balance of trade, and hence it is of vital importance that

French exports should be developed. The Common Market, however, while bringing increased obligations, also provides the means of meeting them. The need for increased exports will coincide with fresh possibilities offered by the Treaty: on the one hand the opening of new and assured markets, on the other hand the very fact that imports will increase, thus satisfying a larger share of consumer requirements on the home market and leaving more goods available for export.

In this connection, it will be of interest to consider the long-term prospects for each country and hence the likelihood of achieving a balance between them, by comparing the allocation of the national product in the six countries, particularly from the point of view of investment.

The following table, giving the allocation of the national product in the six countries in 1954, shows that there was a danger of long-term imbalance if the gross fixed capital formation (*i.e.*, investments) continued to show such wide discrepancies.

	Germany (Fed. Rep.)	*France*	*Italy*	*Belgium*	*Netherlands*	*Luxembourg*
Defence	4·3	7·1	4·4	5·0	5·9	3·0
Public administration ..	12·2	7·0	7·0	8·4	8·7	10·8
Private consumption ..	56·1	67·6	69·7	69·0	58·1	59·3
Gross fixed capital formation	21·1	16·2	19·8	15·9	21·7	23
Net redistribution of goods and services	2·9	1·1	1·2	0·3	1·1	2·1

The same table for 1958, reproduced below, shows that the disparity has diminished, particularly between Germany and France, the percentage of gross fixed capital formation having increased in France to 18·5%; Belgium is still some way behind, however.

	Germany (Fed. Rep.)	*France*	*Italy*	*Belgium*	*Netherlands*	*Luxembourg*
Private consumption ..	59·3	66·3	65·5	68·4	58·0	60·2
Public expenditure: ..	13·5	14·5	12·2	11·0	14·4	12·8
(*a*) Military	2·8	5·9	3·8	3·2	4·6	1·9
(*b*) Civil	10·7	8·6	8·4	7·8	9·8	10·9
Gross fixed capital formation	21·9	18·5	20·6	16·3	22·5	24·0
Fluctuation in reserves ..	1·4	1·7	0·7	0·8	0·7	1·8
External balance	3·9	1·0	1·0	3·5	4·4	1·2
Gross national product at market prices	100·0	100·0	100·0	100·0	100·0	100·0

Moreover, in regard to two important potential sources of imbalance – excessive private consumption and the proportion of the national income absorbed in various ways by the Overseas Territories – the operation of the mechanisms of the Treaty may in itself have a beneficial effect by bringing levels of consumption more into line with each other. But the Treaty as at present drafted cannot be expected to produce any substantial equalisation of the various expenditure headings (defence, expenditure in the Overseas Territories, investment) and a solution to this problem must be sought primarily in the sphere of domestic policy. A policy of harmonisation and balance within the Community is most likely to succeed if the economies concerned are already sufficiently similar in strength to require only supplementary stimuli or adjustments through the mechanisms of the Community.

The Treaty often contains only rather general objectives coupled with machinery for effecting minor adjustments. In regard to the Overseas Territories, for instance, the contributions made by the other member-States to the Development Fund will not have the effect of equalising a burden which, in the case of France, may account for three per cent of the national product. The most precise adjustment mechanisms introduced by the Treaty will do little more than reduce disparities or set in motion a tendency towards equalisation. Some particularly marked disparities may be eliminated by harmonisation in social policy. The common external tariff should have the effect of equalising certain elements in production costs, and the common agricultural policy may tend to even out differences in agricultural prices. The Investment Bank is a means of making an effective contribution to the solution of difficult problems in certain sectors of the economy or in limited geographical areas, and this also applies to the Social Fund. All these are by no means negligible factors making for economic equilibrium, or rather for a reduction in disequilibrium. There can be no doubt, however, that in the long run the most essential prerequisites for a new balance within the Community of Six may perhaps be those which are only vaguely mentioned among the objectives of the Treaty, or are not even mentioned at all.

This applies particularly to the way in which the common trading policy is applied to third countries. Both in agriculture and industry the interpretation placed upon this policy will directly affect the internal pattern of the economies of the member States and the establishment of a new balance of production, prices and consumption for the Community as a whole. In regard to investment there is the immediate problem of the possible effect of capital invested in the Community by third countries. The possibilities of attaining an equilibrium between the six countries of the Community may be seriously affected by the decisions of the bigger foreign companies. There is, however, little practical likelihood that a concentration of investment in one or two countries may be used as a means of dominating the markets of the other countries. As regards domestic investment policies within the Community, it remains to be seen whether the existing machinery for consultation will be adequate. This also applies to monetary policy: the possibilities of a lasting equilibrium will depend upon the extent to which member States are really willing to cooperate, and upon the extent to which the aspirations and aims contained in the Treaty are pursued nationally and within the Community.

It must not be supposed, however, that because there are certain gaps in the Treaty it will be impossible to achieve the desired equilibrium. But it is important to understand that this equilibrium will be *political as well as economic*, and that during the stages of the establishment of the Common Market it must therefore be sought in the framework of the institutions. Hence, the importance of the procedures by which decisions are reached must not be underestimated, bearing in mind the fact that the Treaty lays particular emphasis on these procedures in the co-ordination and harmonisation of general policy.

Although in the early stages of the application of the Treaty there are possiblities of unilateral action, and decisions can generally be taken only by unanimity, this requirement is later abandoned – quickly or slowly according to the importance of the decisions involved – and by the third stage of the transition period, or *a fortiori* after the full establishment of the Common Market, decisions will usually be taken by a qualified majority. This is fundamental to the structure of the Treaty and it reflects the determination of the six signatories of the Treaty of Rome to achieve a true

Community with the widest possible scope. But it would be somewhat unrealistic to imagine that even with the carefully worked-out system of weighted voting certain countries could really impose on another country, at any stage in the application of the Treaty, a course of action in matters of importance which ran seriously counter to that country's views and interests. In fact, of course, the only reason for abandoning unanimity is to encourage compromise by giving a guarantee that a solution to the problem at issue will somehow be found. The rule of unanimity enables a country to obstruct a decision; the rule of majority voting is intended to prevent this obstruction, but the vote of the country concerned still cannot be ignored.

In other words no voting procedure will do away with the need for national and international equilibrium. The rule of majority voting is an expression of political purpose, but it is also based on a feeling of confidence in the salutary effects of the Common Market on the six countries as a whole.

* * *

It will be all the easier to establish the new economic equilibrium at a higher level if the operation of the Treaty has the desired snowball effect on economic expansion.

Mention has been made of the rather striking disparity between the total figures for the production and trade of the Six (a total which places them on a level with the United States) and the figures for their income or consumption, which are far behind those of the United States. May not the reason for this disparity, or backwardness, lie precisely in the fact that the United States already constitute a common market, whereas the Six are still separate? If the economic resources and business activity of the six countries are still not fully reflected in the standard of living of their people, may not the fault lie precisely in this division? Since the establishment of the Common Market is intended to secure the elimination of this general cause of *waste of effort*, there may be a considerable economic expansion which will facilitate the necessary adjustments. Such adjustments are difficult, or even impossible, during a period of stagnation or recession, but they take place automatically and without any difficulty during a period of expansion. The best hopes for equilibrium in the Common Market are thus to be found in the expected expansion of the Common Market itself.

CHAPTER XII

Application of the Treaty

IN its first year of application (1958) the Treaty of Rome did not involve any commercial commitments: that year was to be devoted to the setting up of the institutions and the preparation of subsequent measures. For this purpose the European Commission (2 French, 2 German, 2 Italian, 1 Dutch, 1 Belgian, 1 Luxembourger) was appointed for a period of four years, and proceeded to recruit its staff and establish its provisional headquarters in Brussels, pending the definite selection of a 'European capital'. At the same time the Council of Ministers and the other bodies were set up, thus completing the pattern of the institutional mechanism in its varying aspects: preparation of decisions, consultations, decisions.

The following years, on the other hand, brought very precise commitments both with regard to the member-States (lowering of trade barriers) and the institutions of the Common Market (clarification of the commercial provisions of the Treaty and definition of the basis of the future common policy in other fields). On the whole it can be said that the Treaty has worked well and that the planned programmes have been carried out in full. It is also noteworthy that the main problems have not arisen in those sectors where they were most expected or even feared.

THE CUSTOMS UNION

The step-by-step application laid down in the Treaty, and the various escape clauses, bore witness to a certain caution. In fact, it has proved possible to apply the provisions of the Treaty without undue difficulty, and even to accelerate their application.

The first 10% reduction in *customs duties* between member-States was brought into operation on the 1st January, 1959. The actual incidence of this reduction was not very pronounced and it varied considerably. In Germany the reduction was still below the 25% 'prosperity' cuts which had already been applied from August 1957 onwards. The preference offered to their partners by France and Italy has been reduced by a certain extension in favour of third countries (as long as their duties remain higher than the common customs tariff). In Benelux, the reduction has had very little effect as regards other member-countries, owing to the low level of duties. Finally, early in 1959, some countries replaced certain revenue-raising customs duties by internal taxes so that consumers have not fully felt the effects of the reduction.

The second 10% reduction took effect on the 1st July 1960. It has appreciably intensified the effects of the first reduction and has had the effect of increasing from one-third to one-half the proportion of trade now benefiting from net preferential tariffs. Although the Treaty had provided for flexibility in the application of the reduction, the member-States, at the Commission's suggestion, waived their rights, and the reduction was applied to all products without any exceptions.

At that time it probably seemed that the planned tempo was too slow and that the Treaty, far from setting the pace for economic development, was following in its wake. An important decision was therefore taken on the 12th May, 1960, which accelerated the abolition of customs duties between member-States by means of an additional reduction in tariffs of 10% (linear); the reduction came into force on the 31st December, 1960. On the 31st December, 1961, another change was made, which reduced tariffs between member-States by 40% in comparison with the 1957 level. A further 10% reduction is planned for the first half of 1962. These various decisions are expected to lead, by 1963, to a 60% reduction in internal tariffs and to the second step on the road towards the common external tariff. This will mean, in effect, that developments will be some three years ahead of the timetable laid down by the Treaty.

In the field of *quotas*, the implementation of the Treaty has been still further accelerated. It has proved possible to move forward from the enlargement of existing quotas, as provided for in the Treaty, to complete liberalization, and the actual principle of quotas has been abolished. In the first two years of operation of the Treaty, the proportion of trade liberalised in the various member countries had been raised to between 92 and 98% (O.E.E.C. figures). Two enlargements of remaining quotas had also been carried into effect on the 1st January, 1959 and the 1st January, 1960. We have already mentioned the decision to accelerate, which was made on the 12th May, 1960, and which constituted a considerable advance: all remaining quantitative restrictions on the movements of industrial products between member-States were abolished as from 31st December, 1961.

The enlargement of quotas was also applied to agricultural products and foodstuffs, provided that they did not come under the control of a national marketing organisation. In fact, the quotas which were still of some importance prior to the decisions on the common agricultural policy taken in January, 1962, applied to trade in agricultural products and to the sectors of the economy directly controlled by the State (State monopolies). In 1959, a long-term contract had been signed between France and Germany in regard to certain types of wheat and cereal feeding stuffs. Global quotas for agricultural products were still further enlarged in 1961, and temporary solutions were found in the case of national monopolies such as tobacco. Where difficulties had arisen, the Common Market Commission saw to it that the provisions of the Treaty were strictly applied. Certain applications for exemption by member-States were refused, after very careful examination. Three appeals were submitted to the Court of Justice.

Parallel with the abolition of internal tariff barriers, the customs union involves the setting up of the *common external tariff*. The first task was to complete this tariff where it had not been determined by the Treaty. In February, 1960, the Council approved the tariff in its final form, on the basis of the rules of the Treaty. In March, 1960, the Council approved the rates to be applied to products on list G, important or very sensitive products which gave rise to difficult economic problems, on which it had proved impossible to reach a decision within the framework of the Treaty itself; these products made up some 16% of the trade of member-States. The solution of all these difficulties within the specified time was considered a real achievement.

The common customs tariff which, it will be remembered, is based on an arithmetical mean, is a moderate one. Its weighted average rate is 7·4% (negligible in the case of raw materials, 5·9% in the case of finished goods, 13·6 to 17·2% for capital equipment and other manufactured products). To take an example, the weighted average is 5 points below that of the British tariff in the case of capital equipment and 2 points in the case of other manufactured products.

The decision to accelerate, which was taken on the 12th May, 1960, bringing the reduction of internal customs duties to 30%, involved the first anticipatory step towards the common external tariff. This is an essential symbol of the solidarity of the Six and of their unity *vis-à-vis* the outer world. At the same time, in order to give concrete expression to the liberal attitude of the Community towards third countries, and to minimise their potential problems, it was decided that this first move towards co-ordination should be made on the basis of a common tariff reduced by 20%.

Moreover, it appeared that in many cases, such as the definition of the finishing trades and the marked variations in quota policy *vis-à-vis* certain third countries in cases of abnormal competition, the essential principle of the Common Market – the need for a customs union and for a customs union strengthened by a common trade policy – was fully vindicated. This is particularly true in regard to the dangers which would arise if member-States resorted to protective measures (Article 115) which would hamper the full functioning of the internal mechanisms of the Common Market; such measures would be justified if there were varying conditions of entry for the products of third countries.

Under the Treaty a *common trade policy* was only to be introduced at the end of the transition period. In fact, however, it proved necessary to tackle these problems at a much earlier date. Certain procedures have now been introduced to regulate the relationships between individual member States and third countries: prior consultation about bilateral agreements, co-ordination of the period of operation of these agreements, and the inclusion of a so-called 'E.E.C. Clause' allowing for the revision of the agreement if this should prove necessary in the interests of the Community

But the establishment of the customs union, even when supplemented by a trade policy, was conditional upon the achievement of fundamental progress in agriculture and was legally bound up with the transition to the second stage; the latter depended in turn on the general progress of the Treaty, particularly in regard to the economic union.

Agriculture

Here, the Treaty had laid down objectives and general lines of procedure, stating that the fusion of markets was to be carried out within the framework 'of a common agricultural policy'. After long and difficult discussions, the Council of Ministers of the Community succeeded in giving definite shape to this common agricultural policy on the 14th January, 1962. The aim of this policy is to establish the *free movement of agricultural products in a single market over a transitional period of seven and a half years*. Its other basic elements include the conception of a *uniform* system of protection *vis-à-vis third countries*, *a progressive co-ordination* of prices among member-States with the aim of achieving a single European price, and finally, an assumption of *responsibility by the Community* for certain financial burdens connected with agriculture.

The most important objective is undoubtedly that of achieving a *single price* for a given product over the European market as a whole. In the case of certain products the unification of prices will be brought about mainly by the increased play of supply and demand resulting from the progressive opening of frontiers. For other products, particularly cereals, a special procedure has been laid down, embodying various price-fixing methods. (The 'indicative price' is the basic price of cereals fixed before sowing and intended to come into force when marketing begins. The 'intervention price' is the farmers' guaranteed price during marketing; it will be slightly below the indicative price. The 'threshold price' is calculated by reference to the difference between the home price and the import price, and it serves as a basis for fixing the 'levy'.) This price policy will be the basic factor in the guidance of agricultural production and the maintenance and expansion of farmers' income. The other arrangements which have been adopted must also be regarded in the light of this objective of a single internal price; this applies in particular to the measures for ensuring a uniform rate of protection against imports from third countries (the 'levy').

For the principal agricultural products a graduated levy (equal to the difference between the price in the exporting country and the price in the importing country, and reduced by an amount agreed among the member-

States) will *replace all other national measures of protection* (customs duties, quotas, etc.). This levy will cease to be applied between member-States at the end of the preparatory period in 1970, when uniform prices have been achieved. Export bonuses, calculated in the same way as the levy, will enable a member-country with a higher price level to export products to other countries within the Community, or to third countries.

Another system of levies will be instituted, but in this case at the external frontiers of the Community. It will amount to the difference between the price in the importing country (or, at the final stage, the uniform price) and the world price or, more exactly, the price at the frontier of the importing country including the cost of insurance and freight (C.I.F. price). In the definitive period there will therefore be a single price within the Community, and imports from third countries will be unrestricted but will take place at a price which involves no danger of disturbing the home market price.

The price policy will guarantee farmers an adequate income, but it must not be allowed to lead to overproduction in Europe. It must therefore be accompanied by some control of production within the Community, and this may involve a certain amount of specialisation. *A European Control and Guarantee Fund* for agriculture has been established which will be included in the budget of the Community. The basic purpose of this fund will be to finance interventions on the market (including the export market), but it will also finance activities designed to achieve the objectives of the common agricultural policy, in particular structural changes in the production and marketing of agricultural products. The fund's contribution to the overall cost of the agricultural policy will increase progressively up to the final stage. Contributions will be calculated partly from the budgetary scale laid down by the Treaty, and partly in proportion to each member-country's imports from third countries. It has also proved necessary to make provision for certain protective measures to meet the case of serious disturbances to the markets of particular countries. This system of escape clauses is interesting in that it introduces a new procedure and gives the Commission a very important task. In this field it is particularly difficult to legislate in advance or to foresee all the cases which may arise in practice, and it is left to the Commission to assess the situation and pass a verdict on the suitability of any steps which member-States may have taken. The Council of Ministers will have a sort of 'appeal' function and will be able to reverse the decisions of the Commission by a qualified majority.

In working out their common agricultural policy, the member-States have introduced some interesting developments in regard to the *institutions*. It is true that the normal practice laid down in the Treaty has been followed in the case of certain important political decisions (e.g., the co-ordination of the price of cereals) which have to be taken by the Council of Ministers on the proposal of the Commission, unanimously during the second stage and by a qualified majority from the third stage onwards; but in the case of the escape clauses mentioned above, the normal practice of the Treaty has been to some extent reversed – instead of a qualified majority in the Council being needed to approve the decisions of the Commission, a qualified majority will in future be required to alter them. Finally, five administrative committees are to be set up, each of which will be responsible for one of the main sectors of agriculture. These committees will be composed of representatives of the member-States under the chairmanship of a representative of the Commission. Their duty will be to give the Commission advice or information before it decides on any measures which are to be put into force immediately. Subsequently the Council, as a kind of appeal court, will have the power to amend the decisions of the Commission.

In general, it had become clear that the only way to maintain the balance of the Treaty, to overcome the considerable technical problems arising in the various sectors, and at the same time to allow for sufficient flexibility in the future, was to have full confidence in the working of the institutions and of the Community.

The agricultural policy described above applies particularly to the case of cereals. Here, as elsewhere, the general mechanisms have been supplemented by special regulations. For pork, eggs and poultry, a new concept has been introduced, that of the 'overflow price', in order to avoid disturbance in a sector which is very much subject to price speculation. With regard to fruit and vegetables, there will be much less direct intervention on the market, and a common price will be achieved by a progressive liberalisation of trade. This process will start with top-grade products, and the market itself will be organised largely on the basis of a definition of standards of grading. Similarly, as regards wine, one of the guiding principles will be to increase trade as quality improves; this will go hand in hand with the organisation of production.

Transition to the second stage

As a result of these decisions, the Community has been able to take a big step forward. Not only has agreement been reached on the common agricultural policy, which is the essential basis of a unified system of trade and prices in Europe, but approval has also been given to the transition to the second stage of the Treaty of Rome as from 1st January, 1962.

Transition to the second stage was conditional upon the achievement of progress in regard to the Treaty as a whole. In this connection some important decisions had been taken at the end of 1961 in regard to the implementation of the Common Market in non-commercial fields (the right of establishment), in the rules of competition and in social policy (particularly by the granting of equal pay for men and women). We shall examine these various decisions later on in connection with the progress of the economic union.

The main aspect of the transition to the second stage which deserves mention here is, therefore, the working of the institutions. It will be recalled that the end of the first stage was the only point at which all the member-States had a right of veto in regard to the further development of the Common Market. The general implementation of the Treaty of Rome is now no longer subject to this legal danger. Moreover, the rules of unanimity have now been changed in some cases. For instance, in regard to the abolition of restrictions on the right of establishment, and the mutual recognition of certificates and diplomas facilitating entry into non-wage-earning activities, the directives which previously had to be approved unanimously by the Council, now require only a qualified majority in order to take effect. The same applies to directives regarding the elimination of existing disparities between the legislative, regulatory or administrative arrangements in member-States which run counter to the conditions of competition in the Common Market and cause distortions. But the most important effect of the transition to the second stage is undoubtedly the fact that it leads automatically to the end of the second stage, which will itself signal a more general change in the methods of reaching decisions within the Community; unanimity will then, as a rule, be abandoned in favour of a system of qualified majorities based on proposals made by the Commission.

The economic union

The Treaty of Rome laid down that the freeing of trade should go hand in hand with the establishment of free movement of persons, services and capital, and should be rounded off by the gradual introduction of common policies. In regard to the first point, although the existing obstacles will not be completely abolished until the end of the transitional period, the guiding lines are already clearly laid down in the light of the ultimate objective.

The first regulation concerning the *movement of workers* came into force on 1st September, 1961. It made an important contribution towards the unity of the labour market by eliminating administrative procedures and practices which obstructed the movement of labour 'within the limit of offers of employment actually made' as laid down in the Treaty. It provides for increased facilities for the grant of labour permits and their renewal, improved arrangements for putting applicants in touch with prospective employers, and the co-ordination of certain medical and professional qualifications.

In regard to the free *movement of capital*, a first directive was adopted in May, 1960, which, amongst other things, removes all restrictions on capital movements for direct investment, business dealings and Stock Exchange dealings – in effect, movements of capital connected with the free movement of goods, services and persons. These measures round off and consolidate those which had already been taken at national level in connection with the return to external convertibility of currencies.

October, 1961, saw the adoption of the general programme for freedom of establishment and the free supply of services. It lays down priorities for the removal of restrictions based on nationality which affect the right to take up independent employment. The majority of industrial and commercial activities will be liberalised before the end of 1963 (industry, wholesale trade and reinsurance). During the second stage this will be extended to some of the professions and to the food industry. During the third stage, it will be extended to the medical profession and some branches of insurance, etc. . . . In December, 1961, another very important step was taken towards achieving the effective unity of the Market, and one which involves the concept of a common policy; this was the adoption of the regulation on *industrial agreements*. The basis of this regulation is the principle that all agreements must be registered if their object is the artificial fixing of prices, the limitation of production, markets or investments, market-sharing or the setting-up of barriers to trade between member-States. Application may be made to the Commission for authority to continue existing agreements which are subject to compulsory registration, but new or similar agreements are forbidden, although approval may be sought for them. An advisory committee has been set up, and there are provisions which enable the Commission to undertake investigations in co-operation with member-States and to impose fines or penalties.

The same provisions apply, in general, if an enterprise or a group of enterprises takes improper advantage of a dominant position on the market (cases of monopoly or semi-monopoly), where this is liable to affect trade between the countries of the Community.

The spirit behind these provisions may be defined as the prohibition of improper monopoly agreements and practices, but not of 'good' agreements. The purpose of the regulation, which was adopted on the proposal of the Commission was, in fact, to provide some check on agreements in order to establish whether they are to be considered as good or bad, this assessment being based primarily on their effect. The regulation will enable the executive of the Common Market to implement a global policy on competition, and it can be applied directly in each of the member-States; the legal aspects of this point are worth noting.

Some preparatory decisions have also been taken on the common *transport* policy; in particular, it was decided in 1960 to abolish discrimination in regard to price and conditions of transport on traffic within the Community. And in 1961 a procedure was worked out for joint study and consultation in regard to all the important provisions made by States in this field.

The foundations of the Community's *social policy* are the co-ordination of employment policies and the attempt to achieve a greater mobility of labour; there is also the aim of 'levelling up'. Under this heading, the Treaty laid down precise obligations in regard to the introduction of equal pay for men and women. Agreement on this point was reached in connection with the transition to the second stage. By 30th June, 1962, any differences in pay in excess of 15% are to be brought down to this figure. By 30th June, 1963, differences of more than 10% will be brought down to this figure. By 31st December, 1964, all discrimination has to be abolished. The member-States also reached agreement on more precise definitions and on criteria to be employed for the application of this principle. The Commission will ensure that these obligations are respected.

A common system of social security for migrant workers was established as long ago as 1959, and progress has been made in speeding up the vocational training of certain workers from one member-State who are due to be employed in other member-States. Finally, the Social Fund provided for in the Treaty has been established, and in 1961 the first requests for payment were received in connection with the re-training and resettlement of workers within the Common Market.

There have been two lines of development in *economic policy*. In the first place, two advisory committees – a monetary committee and a committee for economic policy – have co-ordinated the activities of member-States in an effort to combine economic development and monetary stability, and these committees have put forward certain suggestions. Secondly, the Community has laid the foundations of a regional development policy, with the European Investment Bank playing an important part by means of its loans for the development of the less developed regions within the Common Market.

Mention should also be made of the Community's activities within the framework of the Treaty in regard to the *associated overseas States*. Although trading arrangements with the Community are of limited effect (particularly in comparison with the remaining national arrangements), the Investment Fund, having got into its stride, has devoted increasingly large sums to development programmes and now represents an important factor in the economic and social development of Africa, in particular. Incidentally, the efficacy of commercial measures and the balance between commercial measures and financial intervention are among the important questions to be considered when the time comes for the convention to be renewed in 1963.

Overall results

After four years of operation of the Treaty, it is undoubtedly in the economic field that a balance can most easily be struck. In general, it may be said that since the Treaty of Rome came into force the Community has been an area of particularly high economic activity.[1]

Business firms have become clearly aware of the possibilities offered by the Common Market. There are today more than 200 trade organisations covering the Common Market, and numerous agreements between firms from different countries of the Community. Anticipation of the effects of the Treaty, added to the actual effects, has led to a marked upsurge of economic activity in numerous sectors and has given rise to many structural reforms. Agreements on specialisation have been reached. Concentrations and mergers have taken place. Increased investment has enlarged the productive capacity and efficiency of business firms.

In this connection, and as part of the general picture of

[1] It is interesting to note that, while still remaining sensitive to the economic situation in the U.S.A., economic development in the Common Market has shown a definite trend towards autonomy or at least towards a less dependent position.

expansion within the Common Market, we must mention the part played by foreign investment. This has increased steadily since 1958, and has now reached 600 million dollars. During these four years more than 500 American firms have established themselves in the Common Market, compared with 180 in the rest of Europe. In 1960 the amount of this foreign capital invested in the Community was divided as follows: more than 50% in Germany, 20% in France, 16% in Benelux and 7% in Italy.

There are various indices by which we can measure the beneficial effects of all these developments on the economic activity of the Community. Between 1957 and 1960 the gross national product increased by 15% in the Community whereas, in the same period, it increased by only 10·8% in Great Britain and 8·2% in the United States.

General Indices of Industrial Production

1958 = 100

	1958	*1959*	*1960*
France	100	104	115
Belgium	100	104	114
Luxembourg	100	104	114
Netherlands	100	112	127
Germany	100	108	121
Italy	100	111	129
Community	100	107	121
United Kingdom	100	107	114
United States	100	114	118

Expansion continued in 1961, although it was less marked than in 1960 (6% in 1961 against 13% in 1960), mainly owing to certain pressures arising from the shortage of labour and, in part, from the lack of productive capacity.

Employment continued to rise. At the same time, the situation on the labour market encouraged a movement of labour from the less productive to the more productive sectors. It also provided a further incentive to the rationalisation of production and the training of workers. Between 1958 and 1960 the national product per head of population increased by 18·1% in Germany, 13% in Italy, 10·4% in Luxembourg and 8% in Belgium. Although wage increases largely outstripped increases in productivity, except in Belgium, they only had a limited effect on prices. Import prices remained remarkably steady. (They increased slightly in Germany and the Netherlands as a natural consequence of the revaluation of the mark and the florin.) In general, price stability did not suffer as a result of the brisk expansion in demand both at home and abroad.

General Index or Retail Prices

(Monthly average) 1958 = 100

	France	*Belgium*	*Luxembourg*	*Netherlands*	*Germany*	*Italy*
1958	100	100	100	100	100	100
1959	106	101	100	102	101	100
1960	110	102	101	103	102	102

The fact that prices remained relatively steady was partly due to the operation of the Treaty itself in lowering tariffs and to the accelerated supplementary tariff reductions. Nevertheless, the pressure on home prices, which had already been noticeable, became more marked at the end of 1961 and the beginning of 1962, particularly in France.

Purchasing power increased in three years by 18% in Germany, 14% in the Netherlands, 10% in Italy, 9% in

France and 5% in Belgium. (The proportion of the national income going to wage-earners increased particularly in Italy, the Netherlands and Germany.)

But the most spectacular evidence of the results of the Common Market is undoubtedly the development of trade among the countries of the Community itself. There has been a constant and rapid increase by comparison with 1958: *by the beginning of 1962, it had reached a figure of 73%*.

Moreover, this development of trade within the Community has *not taken place at the expense of trade with third countries*; trade with these countries has also increased, and the Common Market's share in world trade has continued to rise. It is interesting to note that the countries which have benefited most from this increase of exports to the Community are, in general, the European neighbours of the Common Market and Great Britain in particular.

Development of Exports to the E.E.C. Countries

Percentage of total exports from each country

	1958	*1959*	*1960*
France	22·2	27·2	29·8
Belgium / Luxembourg ..	45·1	46·3	50·5
Netherlands	41·6	44·3	45·9
Germany (Federal Republic)	27·3	27·8	29·5
Italy	23·6	27·2	29·6
Community	30·1	32·4	34·5
United Kingdom ..	13·9	14·8	15·3
E.F.T.A.	22·7	23·3	24·0

Taken as a whole, imports from other countries of the world increased by 6% in 1959, 27% in 1960 and 35% in 1961. Exports from the Community to the rest of the world have also increased but, on average, they have increased less than imports. (11% in 1959, 25% in 1960 and 26% in 1961.)

Thus the expansion achieved within the Common Market has led to a very considerable increase in imports from third countries. The pessimistic views put forward in this connection when the Common Market was established have proved to be without foundation, principally because they were based on strictly static ideas, whereas the dynamic element in the Common Market has made its impact on the world as a whole.

EXTERNAL PROBLEMS

Whereas the negotiators were chiefly concerned with its domestic effects, and the articles dealing with external relations were often limited to principles and procedures (Articles 111-237-238 for instance) or declarations of intention (Article 110 . .), in fact, it is in this field of external relations that the most urgent, if not the most serious, problems have arisen, owing to the reactions of other countries, and of other European countries in particular.

The Treaty had still not been ratified when the question of the European Free Trade Area was raised; this was a British project to extend to seventeen countries within the O.E.E.C. the internal trade arrangements of the Common Market, but without its economic and political obligations.

The principles involved were in fact radically different. But apart from any question of philosophy, the proposal endangered the future of the Common Market, its momentum and its political development, and also *the practical possibilities of putting it into application*; there was a danger that the imperfections or gaps in a system designed for seventeen countries (diversion of trade, control of origin, exclusion of agriculture, absence of a common policy, etc.) might be reflected in difficulties within the Six and might thus prevent their own integration. But there was also a misapprehension as to the very nature of the Common Market. There was an idea that it was merely a type of trading arrangement which could easily be incorporated in another trading arrangement on a larger scale, and a refusal to admit the need for any economic or political agreements in order to carry out to their final conclusion the trade agreements themselves.

Negotiations in the Maudling Committee were suspended in December 1958. In March 1959, the European Commission published a memorandum setting out all the problems of foreign policy facing the Common Market. This memorandum suggested the following possible lines of approach:

> economic integration could be extended to other countries provided that the latter accepted certain principles and commitments;
>
> failing the conclusion of a long term agreement of this type, trade relations could be improved between the Common Market and all its neighbours, particularly its European neighbours, by a liberal reciprocal policy which would be mutually advantageous.
>
> The Common Market should adopt a common trading policy towards all third countries. In particular, trade discrimination between Europe and the U.S.A. was no longer justified and the problem of relations with parts of the world which were in process of development should not be neglected.

These are the general lines along which the Community has developed. Various new factors have arisen which have fitted into this framework, the most important of these being undoubtedly the resurgence of Europe as a whole and, in particular, the restoration of the balance in the relative positions of Europe and the dollar area. One of the consequences has been the return to convertibility. This is why the measures of liberalisation taken by the Community in favour of third countries have been extended to all the member-countries of G.A.T.T.; discrimination in favour of certain areas or against certain areas no longer has any legal, economic or political justification.

Thus, whereas the first enlargement of quotas had benefited the European countries only, the second increase was made for the benefit of all. The same applies to the lowering of tariffs, a partial extension of which has been decided upon.

These measures for the benefit of third countries are in line with the liberal policy announced by the Community. For our trading partners there is no longer a quota problem in the industrial field. As for the tariff problem, this is a question of level and not of principle. In addition to the measures already mentioned, the Community had declared itself ready to carry into effect, on a reciprocal basis, important tariff reductions, particularly by agreement with the European countries of the 'Little Free Trade Area' set up at Stockholm under the aegis of England in November, 1959, with the object of eliminating or minimising any real trading difficulties which might arise from the varying European tariff systems. These negotiations are to be co-ordinated with those carried on in G.A.T.T., where the very existence of the

Common Market has led to a revival of negotiations for world-wide tariff reductions.

To begin with, tariffs were reduced on certain items at the time when the common tariff was being approved by the Contracting Parties. Then, in 1959, the American Under-Secretary of State Dillon proposed wider negotiations on reciprocal tariff reductions; these have recently resulted (March, 1962) in an agreement between the E.E.C. and the United States, under which the Community is to reduce its tariff by 20% on a number of items. It must be remembered that, when the decision was made to accelerate the establishment of the Common Market, it was agreed that the first move towards coordination should be made on the basis of a common tariff reduced by that percentage. The Community had thus, as it were ,'advanced' concessions on account within the framework of the previous negotiations with G.A.T.T. Other agreements were to follow which would enable this reduction to be extended still further. Discussions have been opened on the delicate problem of trade in agricultural products.

Membership of the Community still remains open to any countries wishing to embark now on a more precise and more binding long-term solution. Under Article 238 of the Treaty of Rome, two European countries, Greece and Turkey, had applied for association as early as 1959. The agreement for association with Greece was signed in Athens in July, 1961. It establishes a customs union between Greece and the Community with certain temporary exceptions in favour of Greece (justified by the underdeveloped state of its economy, which prevented it from adopting the normal tempo of the Treaty of Rome), and a special system of institutions. This arrangement can be summed up from the technical and political point of view as a series of commercial and financial measures intended to enable Greece to bring its economy up to the level of that of the member Countries, with the prospect of acquiring full and complete membership at a later date.

But the most important development in the Community's foreign relations is undoubtedly concerned with the attitude of Great Britain. On 9th August, 1961, Great Britain asked for negotiations with the Community to study the possibility of joining it under the terms of Article 237. These negotiations, which are taking place at the present time, involve the examination of a number of problems, some of which have been explicitly mentioned by the British Government (relations with the Commonwealth countries, agriculture, relations with the member countries of E.F.T.A). Much is at stake, not only for Great Britain but also for the future of the Community and its place in the world. The opening of negotiations with Great Britain was the signal for a series of other applications. Denmark applied for admission to the Community on 10th August, 1961, and Ireland on 31st July, 1961. Three neutral members of E.F.T.A., Switzerland, Sweden and Austria applied at the end of 1961 for commercial and economic association. At the beginning of 1962 Spain also put forward an application. Similar approaches are expected from other countries.

Early in 1962 President Kennedy's American administration took the very important decision to ask Congress for additional powers to enter into new tariff negotiations with the Community which would make it possible to go beyond the traditional methods and achievements of G.A.T.T. and to effect a reduction of tariffs of 50% or more by means of reciprocal agreements on a world-wide basis.

The question of the entry of Great Britain is thus particularly important because it is linked to a considerable extent with other negotiations which are likely to determine not only the structure and size of the Common Market but also some of its political aspects, and to establish a new conception of economic relations in the free world.

* * *

The year 1962 may be said to mark the beginning of an extremely important period for the Community.

So far, the various economic agents have to a considerable extent anticipated the achievement of the Common Market, and their individual reactions have created the conditions which have ensured a rapid development of the economy and of trade (and this itself has opened the way to an acceleration of the Treaty). It must be noted that psychological factors have played a large part in these developments. The expansion which has taken place within the framework of the Common Market and which has favoured its internal development and its relations with third countries, cannot be regarded as a purely automatic outcome of the detailed provisions of the Treaty. The Treaty can be said to have offered a *particularly favourable framework and a wider opportunity* for expansion, to the extent that it provided the means of strengthening dynamic possibilities which were already in existence. It is certain that the continued implementation of the Treaty will also depend on the same set of psychological factors. But the practical effects, which stem directly from the provisions of the Treaty, will undoubtedly increase in importance as the total abolition of customs duties draws nearer.

And now, with the transition to the second stage, the time has come when the Common Market is moving beyond questions of tariffs and trade in the strictly industrial field and is entering the realm of common policies (agriculture, social policy, competition . . . etc.) which, as we have several times pointed out, are of great importance for its balance, its future shape and the achievement of its ultimate objectives.

This is also the point at which the Community's system of institutions will be required to play a predominant part. The Treaty had established a balance between the various organs of the Community, and very active co-operation has been achieved among them. The activities of the Commission itself have developed on two main lines. On the one hand, as the 'watchdog of the Treaty', it has had to take independent action in a number of cases to ensure the observance of certain rules or to enforce the provisions of the Treaty (escape clauses, granting of tariff quotas . . . etc.). In addition, and this is perhaps the most important aspect, it has played a very active part as an initiator – as it was required to do under the Treaty – and it has frequently framed proposals or sketched out guiding lines along which the Governments of the member-States have worked before taking the final decisions which were their prerogative. On the whole, it may be said that this system of institutions has worked well and justified the hopes placed on it, bearing in mind the nature of the problems which arose during this first phase. But some thought is already being given to the problems which may arise in the later phases. Means are being sought to strengthen actual political co-operation among the member States; and studies are being made and suggestions put forward in regard to the composition and powers of the European Assembly, with a view to giving an immediate increase in direct parliamentary control.

Finally, the Community is now engaged in negotiations, particularly with Great Britain, which may have important economic and political implications; and the other industrial giant, the United States, has declared its willingness to embark upon a resolutely liberal policy in agreement with the Common Market. The impact of the Community's agricultural policy on foreign relations, and the framing of a new convention of association with the developing States of Africa and Madagascar, are two basic factors in the Common Market which must inevitably bring about some clarification of the Community's rôle in the world. Again, the possible entry of Great Britain, with all the problems of the Commonwealth which are involved, is a factor which will tend to increase the world-wide importance of the development of the Common Market and which puts further emphasis on the question of relations with third countries. Whilst there is a danger of confusion which might lead to the overlapping or co-existence of complex trading systems, these very problems present an opportunity: the possibility that a strengthened Community may bring a new factor into international co-operation which will lead all the industrial countries to adopt a greater measure of free trade and result in a more satisfactory pattern of trade in agricultural products and better relations with the developing countries.

There can, in fact, be no clear definition of the role of the Common Market in the world without a steady clarification of the nature of the Common Market, i.e., the conception which its own members have of it.

CONCLUSION

From Economics to Politics

THE first concern of the Treaty of Rome is to create a vast market of 170 million consumers, with all the technical and economic advantages which this can be expected to offer. The experiences of the early years have been favourable. But the psychological aspect must be recalled. If the Common Market is to work well – i.e., if advantage is to be taken of the new opportunities and if the desired economic effects are to be achieved, it is essential that public opinion, and especially the various economic agents, should believe in the success of the Common Market. This point is fundamental. The creation of the Common Market will only be worth while if each individual is aware of the opportunities it offers and makes the necessary effort to take advantage of them, so that the whole process takes shape; and each individual will have this awareness and make these efforts only if he feels himself to be engaged in a serious, constructive venture, which will not stop half-way.

One of the essential problems then is that of *guaranteeing* that the Common Market will be achieved. If the Common Market is to be successful, its full implementation must be a certainty right from the start; and to give this guarantee the negotiators of the Treaty felt that a certain number of constituent factors were indispensable, factors which can be grouped under the general heading of integration. The first essential is to embrace all sectors of the economy, in other words to have a global treaty which provides a permanent mechanism of compensation or restoration of balance between the various elements in economic life. Otherwise, difficulties in one particular sector might block progress in another sector. In addition, governments must guarantee to take the necessary measures of harmonisation required for the attainment of the general objectives; that is the second fundamental element in the Treaty. The adoption of a common external tariff is the first of the disciplines enjoined by the Treaty, but there are others which directly or indirectly condition the operation of all the internal economic mechanisms, even the most purely commercial. However, it is often difficult to establish *a priori* the conditions which will permit such measures of harmonisation or co-operation. This leads to the third fundamental element: the necessity for appropriate institutions, endowed with effective authority, which give some guarantee that, whatever the subject involved, a compromise will be found and a decision taken.

This brings us back to the link, mentioned in the introduction in connection with the origins of the Common Market, between its economic and political aspects; these two aspects are indissociable and complementary, even though the Treaty, juridically, is only an economic treaty. The political aspect is primordial; without the initial political determination there would have been no Common Market. And the political aspect must be present all the time while the Treaty is being put into effect: the mechanisms adopted, even those which are strictly commercial, cannot be brought into play without economic commitments and decisions; economic decisions which, by their magnitude, presuppose an unswerving political determination. Finally, the political aspects will appear again at the *conclusion*: the surest basis for further political progress will be provided by the success of the Treaty at the economic level and the achievement of its objectives – the establishment of a unified market between the Six and the transformation of the six economies into a single unit.

* * *

It may reasonably be said that the underlying concern of the Treaty of Rome is to ensure that its provisions are carried out *in toto* and not abandoned half way. It must be clearly realised that the full economic benefits of the large market will come not at the *start* of the process of tariff reductions but at the *end*. A slight reduction in tariffs is doubtless a good thing in itself, but this minor aid to trade is not likely to bring about the hoped-for structural improvements; these can only be found in complete fusion in a large market. It should also be remembered that if these benefits, even those of a technical nature, are to make themselves felt, the belief must prevail right from the start that the project is to be carried on right to the end. In the same way, at the political level, the benefits accrue not at the beginning but at the end. There can be no thought of really constructive political developments – and certainly not of 'natural' developments – until economic unity has been achieved, i.e., until the mechanisms established by the Treaty have run their full course.

We have stressed the fact that, while it is often easy to start, it is more difficult to continue and still more difficult to finish. Seen in this light, the entire economic, legal and political structure of the Treaty of Rome – which may at times appear somewhat complex or theoretical – is in fact the product of experience and inspired by the most down-to-earth realism. It is therefore a profound mistake to judge the Common Market solely by its commercial aspect or to speak of it as the creation of a 'trading block' in Europe. The underlying idea of the Common Market is that the commercial aspects of the Treaty cannot be kept isolated from the economic aspects (which guarantee the implementation of the commercial aspects) or from the political aspects which stem from the size of these economic commitments.

In other words, there are two valid approaches: one is to follow the traditional style of trade agreement, while the other rests on the principle that *if you wish to go further, then you must go very much further.* Trade agreements exist, but any treaty abolishing all customs duties and all quotas must be more than a mere trade agreement, at least if it is intended that the provisions shall be carried out in full. Moreover, this certainty of reaching the goal, the creation of a new economic unit where the idea of trade discrimination against third countries no longer makes sense, is the sole justification for giving more favourable trade treatment to member-States.

It is true that if the Common Market is to be achieved, member-States must display an unswerving determination; it is also true that the future of the Treaty is not entirely certain, any more than is its role in relation to the rest of the world. This brings us back to politics, and two courses of action appear to be theoretically possible.

If the more automatic provisions of the Treaty are not matched speedily enough by the operation of the procedures for economic and social harmonisation, or in particular, if the establishment of the external tariff, the working out of a common agricultural policy and the elaboration of a common trading policy give rise to difficulties, then the Treaty, shorn of all but its purely commercial elements, will no doubt have difficulty in surviving for its allotted span; and it would thus lose the main justification for its existence *in the eyes of its members and of other countries*. Too wide an extension of the trading advantages alone might have a similar effect. It would rapidly become apparent that the Treaty involved numerous difficulties which were not offset by a common political objective and did not offer any assurance of a satisfactory new economic equilibrium. The geographical area of application would be wider, but the tariff reductions would be smaller, since agreements and concessions which can be made between six countries would be impossible in the case of the larger group; it is probable that the automatic mechanisms operative between the Six would come to a halt at the level which was acceptable to the other countries. There would then be a revival of efforts – for the benefit of the Common Market – to free trade and lower customs barriers on a world scale. This would doubtless be an interesting revival, but it would be bound to yield only limited results, and it would also involve the more or less complete abandonment of the Common Market itself.

On the other hand, the full establishment of the Common Market is in no wise incompatible with a great development of world trade and a contribution to its fullest liberalisation; the contrary is in fact true, provided that the Common Market continues its process of consolidation. *In fact an expanding economy within the Six provides one of the best guarantees that the Common Market will have a beneficial effect on trade relations with other countries as well.*

But this second arrangement implies that the speedy implementation of the more automatic provisions of the Treaty of Rome should be accompanied by a real and complete fusion of economies and that the measures of harmonisation or co-ordination mentioned earlier should be fully operative – i.e., the political will must still exist.

The Common Market, as a new unit, will then be fully able to play its leading role in the achievement, not only of a wider unification of Europe but also of a better balance in world economic relations.

In signing the Treaty of Rome the six countries expressed the intention, in the words of their Chairman, M. Spaak, of going 'faster and further' than the other countries in the process of building Europe. The Treaty, by its first economic effects and the political determination of its signatories, offers the most ambitious and the most harmonious plan for Europe. But perhaps the full establishment of the Common Market will not take twelve years and will not be bound by the present very cautious provisions of the Treaty; it will doubtless prove to be both possible and necessary to go 'faster and further'.

INDEX